"This impressive book from Giridhari Dasa makes it clear why he is a spiritual internet star. This systematic, eloquent book provides valuable guidance for those seeking serious spiritual progress."
– Howard J. Resnick (Hridayananda Das Goswami), PhD in Sanskrit and Indian Studies from Harvard, spiritual leader

"In this book, Giridhari Das offers an invaluable present to humanity. Works such as this are true treasures – manifestations of divine compassion in the service of dharma, the higher purpose. I would also say that The 3T Path is a practical survival guide in difficult times."
– Sri Prem Baba, psychologist, spiritual leader

"Quite an achievement."
– Joshua M. Greene (Yogesvara Das), author, researcher and lecturer

"The 3T Path is a must read. Just by reading it, your life will become better and happier!"
– David Roberts (Mahavira Das), Senior Vice President - Bixolon/Samsung

"I can say that I enjoyed every word and instruction in this magnificent work."
– Enéas Guerriero (Iswara Das), author and life coach

GIRIDHARI DAS

THE
3T
PATH

SELF-IMPROVEMENT
AND SELF-REALIZATION
IN YOGA

ISBN: 978-85-907229-3-9

Ilustrations by: pedroluiss
Ilustratio from page 149: Bruna Lima

Graphic Design project by © Coletivo Editorial
Cover Designer: Mateus Dias
Editor: Carl Herzig
Proofreader: Susan Seidenberg
Layout editor: Camila Loricchio

CONTENTS

INTRODUCTION

The purpose of this book is to offer an easy-to-follow and effective guide to personal transformation and growth so that you can maximize your true potential and make the most of your life. This will be done through a retransmission of the ancient path of self-realization in yoga. I want to give you simple yet powerful knowledge as well as practices and tools to make your life increasingly more joyous, give you greater clarity, and make you stronger, more resilient, and better equipped to deal with life's ups and downs, uncertainties, and anxieties.

These are not empty promises. I have been following this path for a quarter of a century, and I have helped thousands of people to follow it as well. I know what it has done for me, and have witnessed its effect on others over and over again. This is an ancient, tried-and-tested recipe for having a great life and achieving enlightenment.

Full disclosure: I'll be using the G-word – yes, God. Maybe you're okay with that. But if you're not, I get it. I was once an atheist, so I know how discordant the subject can sound. It used to totally put me off. I know that God has been poorly represented and that even now horrible things are being done in His name. But if you haven't had a chance to get to know about God from this ancient devotional-yoga tradition, you might be amazed and relieved with what you learn and experience. So please, don't let the subject of God and devotion put you off just yet.

To achieve enlightenment, you must maximize your well-being here and now. One of the great things about the 3T Path is that it conflates spiritual life with your day-to-day life. It covers a lot of ground, from lifestyle suggestions with benefits that are quickly and easily verified, to deeply esoteric spiritual truths that may take decades of serious practice to experience.

What does 3T stand for? As a spiritual teacher, I try to keep things simple. In distilling the core practices from what can be a confusing and seemingly unstructured spiritual tradition, I arrived at three (3) essential transcendental (T) practices that take one through the process of transformation – the 3T Method. Traditionally there are also three avenues along this transcendental path (the threefold path of yoga) and three approaches for transforming regular mundane activities into transcendental action (karma-yoga).

The strength of the 3T Path lies in its combination of ancient and powerful tools: 1) mindfulness, 2) dharma, 3) inner peace, 4) jnana (knowledge), and 5) bhakti (devotion), together with lifestyle suggestions to maximize your potential and the 3T Method to keep your progress steady. All the parts are powerful in and of themselves, but so much more when combined.

Practice is crucial. Information alone can't help; you need transformation. And transformation happens when information is applied in constant and daily practice. In fact, you should begin right away with the 3T Method, which you'll find at the end of the book. You need not wait until you've finished reading the book to begin. By starting with the essential daily practices, you can immediately reap the benefits of the 3T Path. I'll give you information that you can apply, but it must be practiced daily to have any real, lasting effect. So as you read this book, be aware of the many practical guidelines, especially the sections entitled "Key Concept of the 3T Path." The more of these practices you can incorporate, the more transformation you'll experience.

PART 1
WHAT IS YOGA?

PART 1 - WHAT IS YOGA?

A Trip through Time

To better understand what yoga is, we have to take a trip through time. Let's start with the present day. Most people's understanding of yoga today is based on the increasingly popular practice of different postures, coupled with relaxation and breathing exercises.

This modern practice of yoga was founded by Tirumalai Krishnamacharya (1888-1989). So, our first stop on our trip is about one hundred years ago, when Krishnamacharya took an interest in the practice of hatha yoga, a form of yoga that relies on the use of physical postures.

Krishnamacharya traveled to a cave in the Tibetan Himalayas to seek instruction from a hatha-yoga guru named Ramamohan Brahmachari, who was reported to have been 150 years old. He lived with his guru for 7 years, studying different postures and Patanjali's *Yoga Sutras*, a 2,000-year-old philosophical treatise on yoga. Ramamohan is said to have mastered 7,000 postures, or asanas as they are called in Sanskrit. Krishnamacharya is said to have mastered 3,000, though he managed to transmit only 640.

Upon returning to society in around 1931, Krishnamacharya brought to the public his knowledge of asanas as a healing technique and means of promoting physical well-being. His innovation was to present asanas as an easily taught and easily learned and applied technique for good health.

Asanas were no longer merely a tool for mystics on the path of enlightenment, though Krishnamacharya himself was a practitioner of the devotional path of yoga and knew well its full meaning, even though he became famous for teaching the more physical style.

Travelling around India teaching this style of yoga practice, Krishnamacharya quickly became popular. Two of his most famous disciples were B.K.S. Iyengar and K. Pattabhi Jois, both of whom played key roles in bringing the practice to the rest of the world.

So, what most people today understand as yoga is actually a modern practice, not even a hundred years old, which is why academics use the term "Modern Yoga."

Let's go back in time again, to the 1400s, to the founding text of hatha yoga, the *Hatha Yoga Pradipika*. The original form of hatha yoga contained therein makes use of asanas, breathing techniques, and other physical practices, including colon cleansing, with the express purpose of seeking enlightenment, not merely physical well-being. Interestingly, the *Hatha Yoga Pradipika* includes only eleven asanas. It was a practice primarily for solitary male mystics living in nature, near holy rivers or in caves.

Our next stop is the time of Jesus, two thousand years ago, when the sage Patanjali compiled the *Yoga Sutras*. In the *Yoga Sutras* we find almost no focus on physical practices, and not a single asana is mentioned. The entire focus is on the internal, spiritual aspect of yoga—the proper mindset, controlling and observing the mind, how the mind works, meditation, and the final goal of liberation. It's a technical but beautiful treatise on the workings of our consciousness—recommended reading for those who follow the 3T Path.

Our last stop in time will be to the time of Krishna, for whom scholars have no set date, but that tradition and calculations based on astronomical events mentioned in the stories indicate to be about 5,200 year ago. Krishna is the speaker of the most widespread and famous yoga text, the *Bhagavad-gita*, a 700-verse jewel of spiritual wisdom. One of the claims of the *Bhagavad-gita* is that the knowledge of yoga had been lost and that Krishna was bringing it back to the world. The *Bhagavad-gita* is thus the primordial text on the essence of yoga, and one must understand it to truly understand yoga. It shows us yoga as a philosophy of life, a guide to living joyously and a devotional spiritual practice meant to connect the soul to the Divine and transcend material suffering. There is mention of only one asana, a simple sitting posture for meditation.

In the context of the *Bhagavad-gita*, the dictionary meaning of *yoga*, "to connect," makes sense. Yoga means to connect to yourself, or in other words, to be true to yourself, and to connect to the source of all, by means of observing and directing your mind.

The Threefold Path of Yoga in the Bhagavad-gita

As mentioned earlier, 3T also refers to the three avenues of progress on the path of yoga: karma (behavior), jnana (knowledge), and bhakti (devotion). Each of these gets its own chapter in the *Bhagavad-gita*, and together they comprise the basis of Krishna's presentation.

Behavior covers a wide range of ideals and practices. Karma means "action," in Sanskrit, but I am using the term *behavior* because the path of yoga gives us amazing insights into so many practical aspects of our life. The most basic are lifestyle choices. Then there are ethical and moral principles. Another major aspect is the concept of dharma and its application to our day-to-day lives.

This leads us to the third meaning of 3T – the three approaches for transforming mundane activities into transcendental action (karma-yoga). This will be described in a section of its own, as it's of great importance and has an incalculable effect in your well-being and outlook on life.

Next we have jnana (knowledge, pronounced "gyana"), which refers to knowledge on two levels: the practical and the metaphysical – knowledge to help you deal with this world and knowledge to shape your spiritual path. I use the word *wisdom* in this regard, to emphasize that this is the kind of knowledge that will positively change how you react and deal with life. A large section of this book is devoted to transmitting some of these key concepts, and you'll see how they can effect enormous change in your life, in how you define your priorities and your identity. As knowledge strengthens your intelligence and you become wiser, you can, increasingly, guide your life based on rational, well-thought-out, sound decisions.

Lastly there is bhakti (devotion). As I mentioned in the introduction, I can relate to those for whom the subject of devotion is distasteful at this point in his or her life. But one of the beauties of the 3T Path is that it's not all or nothing. You can take what you can now and go with that. Every aspect of the path will help you in your transformation. And as we are transformed, our view of the world, of ourselves, of what we think is important, is also transformed.

It's like growing up. The things we loved doing at age five are not the same as those we like doing as adults. And in terms of transforming your mind, simply reaching adulthood makes little difference. Age no longer matters. It's all up to what effort you put into becoming a better, wiser person. As such, your views on God and devotion can change with new information and new experiences. This yoga tradition is the oldest in the world to address a single, transcendent supreme God, and it brings information on God and devotion to God that is quite different from what most of us brought up in predominantly Christian, Jewish, or Muslim countries have been exposed to.

Even better, because the yoga tradition values good sense, intelligence, philosophy, and rationality, and rejects sectarianism and coercive religiosity, the way it presents and explains God and devotion is more compatible with a modern mindset. Even if you've never felt devotion to God, you may have cultivated devotion to a cause or project and thus have experienced or witnessed how devotion can be a powerful force. It's powerful because it's an expression of your love. Devotion can motivate you like nothing else. It can help you overcome hurdles, encourage you when you are down, and bring out the most of what you have to offer.

Devotion is thus the most powerful tool you have for transformation. In the path of yoga, it's given the highest importance and repeatedly shown to be necessary to maximize your full potential. And ultimately, when it comes to spiritual liberation and enlightenment, it is meaningless to speak of *yoga*, or connection, without addressing the love of the individual for God, as no other connection is more important than love.

Advancement in one avenue strengthens your ability to advance in another. As we improve the quality of our life choices and habits, our mind becomes clearer and more focused. And a clearer, more focused mind is better able to absorb knowledge and more proficient in seeing and understanding the big picture. More knowledge, in turn, helps you become wiser and thus improves your reactions and choices in life.

More knowledge will also bring you more information about God and the soul and thus strengthen and support your devotion. Better behavior also becomes a means to develop and strengthen your spiritual life. At the same time, devotion will inspire you to do better, to be a better person – to improve your behavior. Devotion also brings a natural intuition, making you wiser. And so on. The result is clear: any effort on your part to advance in any one of these avenues will bring about increasing well-being and facilitate further advancement along the path. Putting in effort on all three every day will bring about great positive changes in your life.

In a graphic presentation of the three avenues of perfection, your state of consciousness is represented by a triangle in the middle. The triangle is formed by the degree of advancement in each of the three avenues. The higher the state of consciousness, the better you feel. Practically speaking, happiness is the gauge of advancement. The more you work on yourself, the more you experience bliss – *ananda* in Sanskrit. The more disturbed and dark your consciousness, the more you experience suffering – klesa in Sanskrit. Note that the three avenues meet up at the top. Essentially, perfect knowledge requires perfect behavior, which requires perfect loving devotion. At the top is *prema*, a Sanskrit word used to denote pure spiritual love, the final and most perfect state of existence.

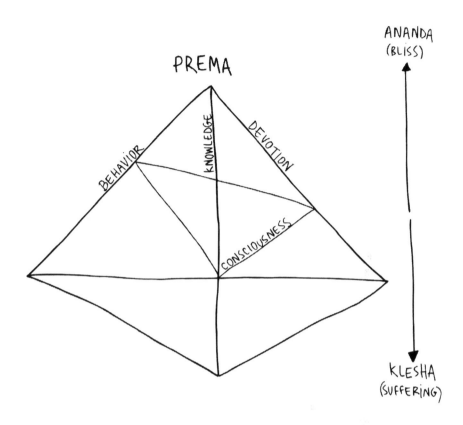

The Yoga of Meditation

"So what about all those postures," you may ask, "those asanas we always see? What are they all about?" No asanas are described in the *Yoga Sutras*, and only one is mentioned in the *Bhagavad-gita*. In both cases the asanas are part of the act of meditation. It is, in fact, important to sit properly with your back straight to better meditate. So there has always been a connection between the posture of the body and yoga, but originally it was for the express purpose of meditation. Meditation is so important, so central to the path of yoga, that from it arises an alternative path of yoga, different from the general threefold path described above. This is known as the yoga of meditation. In the *Bhagavad-gita* it's called dhyana-yoga, as *dhyana* is the Sanskrit word for meditation, and in the *Yoga Sutras* the term *astanga-yoga* is used (not to be confused with the dynamic modern yoga system that goes by the same name).

In dhyana-yoga, the practitioner gives up his or her social life to live secluded in nature, dedicated exclusively to meditation, usually near a sacred river or in a cave. The goal is to immerse the mind in the sharpest, most precise meditation on God, to the point where nothing else can be felt or perceived.

The intensity of the power of meditation, of focus, that such a yogi achieves is beyond our experience and difficult to understand. You have probably been awed by professional athletes at the top of their game and seen them do things you couldn't dream of doing. Imagine what these mind athletes achieved meditating deeply for eighteen or more hours a day for decades on end.

Reports of such yogis living for hundreds of years aren't so hard to believe. After all, these were people living with no stress on a wild, raw, organic diet, slowing down their breathing and heart rate for the better part of the day. Even more amazing are the abundant descriptions of the special powers these meditators could achieve. Levitation, being immune to fire and poison, and suspending breathing for hours were beginner's stuff for them. They are also said to be able to change shape, telekinetically move objects, and bestow curses and blessings. Their range of powers reportedly included producing anything desired; controlling others' minds' assuming any size, from atomic to planetary; multiplying oneself; and teleporting to anywhere in the universe.

These are pretty wild claims. But can we say they are impossible? After all, many of the technological wonders we take for granted today would have seemed impossible less than a hundred years ago. These legendary meditators developed such control of their minds that they could access the very workings of material nature. I like to think of this as a very advanced form of technology. Interestingly, whenever such powers are mentioned in sacred texts, they come with the warning that they are dangerous temptations and will lead to the fall-down of the yogi who misuses or becomes proud of them. Focusing on external reality and material selfish goals, along with the mental agitation of pride and power, can destroy the purity of a yogi's focus and determination.

In short, this path of dhyana-yoga is both difficult and intense. But it's not the one most recommended, or the most efficient, and today it is practically non-existent.

It is not difficult to imagine, however, that with passing centuries, meditators took interest in the effects their postures could have on their bodies. They gradually developed a large library of postures, noting their effects on the mind and body. It's a wonderful by-product of a tradition that has a lot more to offer.

PART 2
THE FIVE AVENUES OF PERFECTION ON THE 3T PATH

PART 2 – THE FIVE AVENUES OF PERFECTION ON THE 3T PATH

After years of practicing and teaching self-realization in yoga, I became aware that I could better practice and explain this path by expanding the three traditional avenues of behavior, jnana (knowledge), and bhakti (devotion) into five. I call them "the five avenues of perfection of the 3T Path." **The five avenues of perfection are mindfulness, dharma, inner peace, jnana (knowledge), and bhakti (devotion).** I broke up "behavior" into two major avenues – mindfulness and dharma – and I added a fifth element, inner peace, which is related to behavior and knowledge. Improvement in each of these five can bring huge positive changes in your life. Dedicating yourself to all five of them will bring about a remarkable transformation.

KEY CONCEPT OF THE 3T PATH
It's All About the Mind

Your entire life experience is 100 percent dependent on your mind. This cannot be overemphasized. I know it can be hard to accept at first, but the more you delve into and invest in this path of interior transformation, the more you'll experience it. On one end of the spectrum is the crass materialist who thinks that happiness and well-being is dependent on external reality – where he or she is, with whom he or she is, and what things (possessions, money, social status, looks, . . .) he or she "owns."

On the other end of the spectrum is the self-realized yogi, who is in constant and profound bliss regardless of the external situation. The difference? The mind. It's not about the external reality, but about how you interpret it.

Of course, it's a long road from one end of the spectrum to the other. The good news is that you will experience results at every step. The even better news is that this is for real. People have been doing it since before the building of the pyramids of Egypt. Not only do we have testimony from generation after generation of yoga practitioners, but now we have the neuroscience to back it up. And you can experience it yourself, right from the beginning, following the 3T Path.

The core issue is your ability to focus your mind, and what you focus it on. The sage Patanjali put it perfectly: "Yoga means to control the functions of your mind." The five avenues of perfection of the 3T Path are all about this, explained in such a way as to make it accessible for anyone in this day and age.

Mindfulness

Mindfulness is a modern term for one aspect of this ancient yoga practice. In short, it means to be aware, to be conscious of your consciousness, and to be able to experience a thought, sensation, or external action with your full attention. This requires a lot of practice, because most people just get lost in thought. Research shows that we have about seventy thousand thoughts a day![1] Just sitting down for breakfast, you play out different imagined scenarios, engage in a non-stop mental conversation, weigh the pros and cons of this or that, replay and review the movie you saw last night, . . . In a matter of seconds your thoughts can stray from an encounter you had the other day to plans of what to do tonight to being anxious about an upcoming meeting at work. This has been going on for much of your life, and it will continue if you don't start doing something about it.

The Source of All Our Misery

What's wrong with having your thoughts run out of control – with not being aware of what you're doing here and now? The main problem is that you're driving yourself crazy. Anxiety, fear, depression, anger, frustration, and confusion are just a few of the symptoms we experience when we lose control of our thoughts.

One of the tricks your mind likes to play with you is mental time travel. We look to the past and lament over events, conversations, and choices. We rehash failed relationships, conversations gone wrong, and bad life-choices, or else lament over how much better thin-

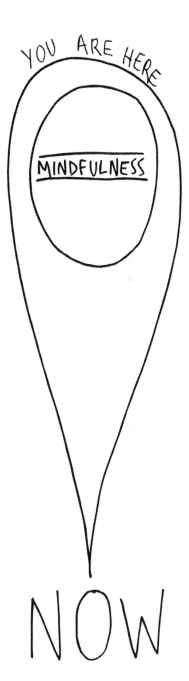

1. *Laboratory of Neuro Imaging at University of South California website*

gs used to be. When you relive an unpleasant experience or focus on what you don't have now that you had before, the result is the same: misery. You subject yourself to negative sensations, reinforcing and strengthening them.

Even more common is travelling to the future and updating your list of what you need to be happy. This is called "conditional happiness," telling yourself that you'll be happy only under certain conditions, all of which are in the future. You'll be happy when you go to college, when you get a job, when you get a promotion, when you get married, when you have children, when you get fit, when you buy a new TV or phone or car, and on and on.

Conditional happiness is a trap, a no-win situation. The big problem is that you're telling yourself that you are incomplete, unhappy, or not yet "there." Even though you don't mean to put yourself down, by telling yourself that you'll be happy when this or that happens or when you get this or that thing, you're saying that you're not happy now – you're not satisfied or complete.

And it gets worse, because as soon as you place your bets on some future, external thing or situation to be happy, you can't help but feel anxious about it. Consciously or not, you'll get anxious about when it will come or anxious that it won't happen at all. You'll feel frustrated that you don't yet have it, and you'll feel angry if something happens to push that reality further into the future, or to make it unfeasible.

If all these feelings of dissatisfaction, anxiousness, frustration, fear, and anger aren't enough to ruin your day, here's the final blow: when you do achieve one of the items in your conditional-happiness list, the positive feeling is short-lived, sometimes practically non-existent. Maybe graduating from high school was a big item on your list. But for how long after graduation day were you actually happy? Getting into college? How long did that sustain your well-being? Getting your first job? Your new car? New phone? How long did you feel satisfied, complete, realized, or happy upon achieving these goals? What probably happened is what happens with most of us: as soon as you got one item in your list, you updated your list and didn't feel so amazing after all. Your mind gave you no rest, no satisfaction, no lasting joy.

Bad Company

Imagine being stuck with a babbling, negative person – someone who just will not shut up, not even for a second. And what this person is saying is far from entertaining, valuable, or necessary. It's mostly drivel and stuff to make you feel bad about yourself. That would be very unpleasant, wouldn't it? But does it sound familiar? It should. Because I'm talking about your uncontrolled mind.

From the second you wake up, your mind starts going on about this or that, rehashing past events, babbling nonsensically, and pressuring you to fulfill your conditional-happiness list. What's worse, your mind likes telling you horror stories. It wants you to know the many ways you're going to fail and the horrible consequences that will ensue. If you have a college exam, or a business presentation, it's going to question how likely it is that you're going to fail. And if you fail, what kind of a future will you have? The mind is so good at this that it can convince your brain to activate your fight-or-flight responses: higher blood pressure, accelerated heart rate, increased adrenaline output, and rapid breathing. And you haven't yet even gotten out of bed!

This is why anxiety is such a widespread phenomenon. You're stressed not because of what you have to do, but because of what your mind is telling you about what you have to do. You allow yourself to become a victim of your mind's unceasing chatter, negativity, and incessant fear mongering.

You have to learn to change this routine gradually, day by day. It turns out you have the power to redirect the mind, to pacify it and to gradually overcome its ability to ruin your life.

First Mindfulness Technique: Here and Now

The first step is to bring your mind to the here and now. As you notice your mind dragging you to the past or future, take a deep breath and bring it to the present. This is a key component to serious transformation. It will immediately improve your life, and it will lay the groundwork for illumination.

One exercise is to focus on any one sensation. Here are some examples: 1) the sun entering your room or warming your skin, 2) a slight breeze blowing, 3) birds chirping in the distance, 4) the wind blowing, rustling leaves, 5) silence, 6) water gliding off your body in the shower, 7) the feel of your sofa or chair, and 8) your breathing.

While breathing deeply and slowly, take control of your mind, direct it to the chosen sensation, and focus your attention on that.

If you can, try this now for a minute, or even less, and see how you feel.

The more you do this, the more proficient you'll become. Studies show that if you do something for three weeks, it becomes wired into your brain as a habit. It's important that you try to do it every day, as many times a day as you can, for at least three weeks so that it becomes a natural part of your day-to-day life.

Here and now are divine, because this is where life is actually happening. The past is gone, and the future does not exist. The more time you spend in the here and now, the more you'll experience life as it really is. It's in the here and now that you'll be able to access ever deeper levels of existence, joy, and spirituality.

One common misconception about being in the here and now is in regard to planning. Obviously you can't have a meaningful productive life if you don't have goals or plans. But planning is an activity to be done here and now. There's a right time for it. Planning is different from fantasizing about a conditional-happiness list. It's one thing to plan for retirement by setting up a financial retirement account and paying into it every month, and quite another to yearn for retirement and fantasize about it as you go to work. Yearning and fantasizing about it will make you miserable. Planning for it and acting upon your plan, but with your mind here and now, will keep you content.

Second Mindfulness Technique: Focus on Your Actions, One Step at a Time

The most important way to keep yourself in the here and now is to fully direct your mind to whatever task is at hand. Let's return to the example of waking up and being barraged by the mind filling you with horror stories and dragging you to the past and future. To pacify your mind, take one action at a time and put your full attention on it. Getting out of bed, for example. Be aware of your bed, your bedroom, how your body feels after sleep, the floor or your slippers, the temperature, the sounds. Perhaps your next move is to go the bathroom. So just do that. One step at a time. No need to be worried about your exam or business presentation if you haven't even had a shower. The more you can keep your focus on what you are doing, here and now, the better you'll do those things and the more pacified and joyous your mind will be. This is a simple but profound technique. Whatever you're doing, bring your mind with you. Do it with your full attention. Be there body and mind, here and now.

Science Supporting Mindfulness

There is a growing library of medical evidence for the power of mindfulness and its positive effects on our mental and physical health.

1. Coronary Artery Disease

   The addition of meditation training to the standard cardiac rehabilitation regimen has been shown to reduce mortality (41 percent decrease during the first two years, with a 46 percent reduction in the rate of recurrence), morbidity, psychological distress, and some biological risk factors (plasma lipids, weight, blood pressure, and blood glucose) (Linden 1996, Zammara 1996).

2. Chronic Pain

   Mindfulness meditation has been shown to reduce both the experience of pain and its inhibition of patients' everyday activities. Mood disturbances and psychological symptomatology (including anxiety and depression) were also reduced. Pain-related drug utilization was decreased, and activity levels and self-esteem were increased. This was in marked contrast to a traditional pain-clinic comparison group, which showed no change in these dimensions (Kabat-Zinn 1982,1985). These gains were nearly all maintained at four-year follow-ups (Kabat-Zinn 1987).

3.   Anxiety

Mindfulness training has been shown to reduce symptoms of anxiety, psychological distress, and secondary depression (Kabat-Zinn 1992). Changes were maintained at three-year follow-ups (Miller 1995).

4.   Depression

Skills derived from mindfulness training and cognitive therapy have been shown effective in significantly reducing the recurrence of major depressive episodes in patients who have been treated for depression (Ma & Teasdale 2004, Segal 2002, Teasdale 2002, Teasdale 2000).

5.   Migraine

Migraine patients who practice mindfulness show a decrease in the frequency and intensity of their migraines (Anastasio 1987).

6.   Insomnia

The practice of mindfulness has led to increases in the quality and pattern of sleep of those suffering from insomnia (Winbush, Gross, & Kreitzer 2007).

7.   Fibromyalgia

Patients who practice mindfulness show significant clinical improvements in their physical, psychological, and social conditions (Kaplan 1993, Goldenberg 1994).

This is a short list. The real benefit is in how you'll feel. You'll experience life with greater peace, more clarity, and less anxiety.

Practice Makes Progress

It's not all or nothing; it's a practice. You'll sometimes lose your mind to future anxieties, past regrets, and idle mental chatter, but then you'll be able to bring it back to the here and now and experience peace. Lose it, bring it back. Over and over again. All day long. For the rest of your life. Over time, you'll get better at it and fall victim to your mind's trick less often. Eventually, it will become second nature. There's a famous section in the *Bhagavad-gita*, where Krishna says that for one who has controlled the mind, the mind is the best friend, and for one who has not, the mind is the greatest enemy. Mindfulness is a key component to making your mind your best friend.

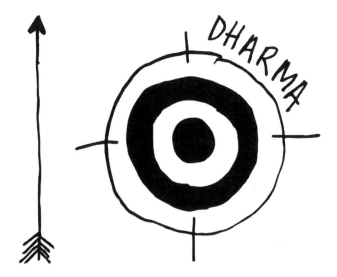

Dharma

Dharma is a rich concept, and the word many meanings, but my focus will be on dharma as that which needs to be done – essence and duty. Duty can be imposed; essence cannot. Dharma is thus that duty born of who you truly are, of your nature. It's not an external or social imposition. It's what you need to do at any given moment to be the best person you can be. It's doing the right thing at the right time. Being dharmic is more than just doing good or avoiding hurtful or violent behavior, though that is certainly included in the concept, and it can't be boiled down to a list of don'ts or things to be avoided. Dharma is fluid and alive and sensitive to different aspects of your life. Major changes to your dharma can occur from one second to the next. One way to understand dharma is to rephrase the classic line: "Don't ask what the world can do for you, but ask what you can do for the world."

Dharma is the guiding principle of life, at each moment showing you what you should do, resolving your doubts as to which course to take, and simplifying your actions. It is your integrity in action and the truthful expression of your being. You'll find your place in the world when you're in tune with your dharma.

Dharma is also an integral part of nature. It's not a psychological or religious concept. The degree to which you are true to your dharma will directly affect how you feel on a day-to-day basis. Being true to yourself means acting according to your dharma. Thus, the more you can remain attuned to your dharma – the more you can act based on it – the more you'll feel satisfied, whole, true, and happy. The more dharmic your behavior, the more you will feel content with who you are now. And the more dharmic your life, the more you can look back at it with joy and a feeling of accomplishment.

Being in the Zone

Mindfulness and dharma go hand in hand. Dharma is so natural that to become increasingly attuned to it you need only remove that which is not natural, foremost of which are selfishness, fear, and greed. If you're a victim of conditional-happiness lists or just lack sufficient awareness of your actions, you'll fail to see your dharma. The perfect focus on the here and now is to focus on your dharma and to put all your attention on performing your dharma to the best of your ability. Even just this will bring immediate and sustained joy. You have already experienced it. You may recall moments when you were totally focused on doing something that was your duty, with no regard to yourself or future rewards or even dangers. Parents, especially mothers with babies, experience this often. It's called being in the zone. Positive psychology (the branch of psychology that studies what makes people happy), points to being in the zone as one of the primary pillars of a happy life. To be focused on the action necessarily implies not being focused on the material benefits or sacrifices that the action will bring about in the future. Focusing on your dharma here and now is the polar opposite of yearning for future results. This is such an important point that Krishna mentions it no less than ten times in the *Bhagavad-gita*. This change of paradigm is the key to experiencing a giant leap in well-being.

KEY CONCEPT OF THE 3T PATH
The Change of Paradigm: Life vs. Fantasy

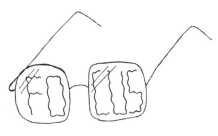

The untrained mind constantly strives to look for external solutions to life, and a person will constantly seek to adjust external reality to suit his or her desires. Lists of conditional happiness are continually updated. The untrained mind will thus spend a lot of time in a fantasy world daydreaming about what seems like a brighter future. Basically, these desires involve changing the future in three ways: 1) getting things, 2) getting people to cooperate with your plans, and 3) hoping for favorable situations to arise. But usually, not much changes when one of these goals is achieved. Desires, once attained, satisfy very little, and other pressing desires soon take center stage. Living like this is one of the components of a terrible life. As explored in the Mindfulness section, when the mind is in the future desiring results, anxiety about future outcomes is unavoidable, as is frustration with life as it is today, anger when apparent obstacles postpone these future desires, and fear that it will all turn out badly. We have all tried to live like this, and it just doesn't work. It has never worked. It is no way to attain peace, contentment, and joy.

We need a change of paradigm. Instead of focusing on the future, on the illusory belief that some combination of external reality (these things, with those people, under that situation) is the key to happiness, we should focus on just living life well, here and now, focused on our dharma. Life vs. fantasy.

Life is happening at every moment. It's in flux — a constant stream of events. The challenge is to be fully present as it's happening. The joy arises from doing your dharma well, here and now, and moving from one dharma to the next. Being the best person you can be today, right now — true to yourself. It's that simple. There is no need (and very little use) to daydream about the future. Reality is more beautiful than any daydream if you learn to access it completely. Future events will unfold under the all-powerful force of time. And life usually plays out very differently from anything you had imagined. This is neither good nor bad; it just is — it's reality. The more we can be attuned to reality, the happier we will be. Instead of imagining that a certain combination of things and people will bring you peace and joy in the future, you should seek to attain peace and joy with life as it is, with the wonderful blessing of being active in your dharma, of being alive right now.

The Seven Dharmas

There are seven basic categories of dharma. There are subtleties, but these seven categories will serve as a strong foundation.

1. Vocation Dharma

The first dharma is for most people the hardest of all. It is your life's calling, your vocation, born of your psychophysical nature. Some people are blessed to know his or her vocation at an early age. I've seen this with dancers, artists, and actors. There are stories of young athletes who stand out when they are young and are guided by parents and teachers to become professionals in their sport. Others gravitate naturally toward academic or scientific work. But for most, it can be a struggle.

Finding one's dharma is so often a struggle because society teaches people from an early age that what they really need is money, with secondary goals of stability and respect. In other words, just about everyone is taught from birth to choose the fantasy paradigm. Instead of teaching people to do what they're good at doing and to help them develop their unique talents and inclinations, normally parents, culture and the school system will treat people like blank slates, giving them a one-size-fits-all education, and encourage them to make as much money as possible.

So here are some tips on helping you find your vocation. Remember, it's never too late.

1. When meditating on what you'd like to do, remove from the equation any external factors. It's about who you are, not about practical concerns.

2. Forget money. Do not think, "I can't do art, because that doesn't pay" or "I can't do philosophy because what kind of a job will I get?" Remove such considerations from your mind. One way to do this is to think, "If I won the lottery, I'd like to work on . . ."

3. Forget social pressure and pride. It's not about what your parents (or anyone else) want you to do. It doesn't matter if there are five generations of military men in your family, if you're not into military life. It's not about social status either. Maybe society doesn't appreciate a janitor or waiter, but these are perfectly noble professions. A person who has the psychophysical nature to do the job of a janitor and is doing it is far better off than the person doing the job of a lawyer but

whose true psychophysical nature is that of a musician. The janitor can easily find peace and joy in his job; the misplaced lawyer will always feel frustrated and unrealized.

4. Don't just think about what you like to do. You may like to do a lot of things. Instead, think what is that one thing you can't help but do. Toward what type of activity do you naturally gravitate?

5. A note for potential educators: Teachers have a double vocation. They first have to accept that they are born to teach, and then they have to find out what it is they are most inclined to teach.

Finding your vocation involves who you are now. There are tools and processes you can use, including vocational tests, talking to people who are close to you, and even Vedic astrology. The best thing is to seriously look into your heart and feel your nature. Spend some time alone, in silence, and do some hard thinking. Be brave and willing to accept your true nature. Don't compromise yourself. And don't let fear of the future stop you.

Finding your vocation is essential. To spend your working hours doing something not suitable to your psychophysical nature will corrode your chances of happiness. It's an offense to your person, like keeping your true self locked away.

2. Natural Dharma

Krishna explains in the *Bhagavad-gita* that a yogi has to satisfy three natural needs: 1) sleeping, 2) eating, and 3) recreation. These form our "natural" dharma, as they are fundamental needs of our body and mind. Krishna emphasizes that one should not eat too much or too little or sleep too much or too little. What's too much? Well, too much for you. We're all different. And what's too much or too little for you will be different at different times in your life. So you have to find your balance. Living your dharma is all about balance, knowing when to switch from one dharma to another. This natural dharma means that you have to take seriously, as a duty, as part of your essence, the simple acts of eating, sleeping, and recreation.

You have to take time to eat, to value that moment. Eating shouldn't be rushed or involve shoving food in your mouth while you're doing other things. It should be treated as a sacred duty, a time to think about your dietary choices and what you're putting into your body. It's the crucial moment of the day when you're replenishing yourself. Is this meal compatible with who you are? Is it really good for you? Is it good for the planet? Serious choices, with serious consequences. In a world where people are killing themselves and destroying the planet with poor dietary choices, it's easy to see eating as one of the core dharmas.

Sleep is not a waste of time; it's an essential component to your mental and physical health. Lack of sleep can have a dramatic negative impact on your health and even cause death (if one falls asleep while driving). It's your duty to make all the necessary arrangements to sleep well and to sleep enough. Sleep should not be that thing you do when you can no longer stay up, or that you interrupt because you're forced to go to work. As it is your dharma, your duty, to sleep enough, you must arrange your life to accommodate this crucial need. Treating sleep as your dharma also means that when you go to bed you should not be thinking about other dharmas, such as work. You should just sleep. Clear your mind and stay in the here and now of just sleeping.

Seeing recreation as one of your dharmas means that you can dispel all sense of guilt when you get time to play or take a vacation. It also means you *should* take time to play and have a vacation! All work and no play makes Jack a dull boy... and also not a very dharmic one. I find it fascinating and reassuring that such an ancient text as the *Bhagavad-gita*, describing what it takes to become enlightened, mentions the importance of recreation.

3. Occupational Dharma

Regardless of whether or not you have found your true vocation when you accept a job, run your own business, or enroll in a full-time program of study, you have accepted a major dharma. I call this the occupational dharma. It's usually the one that demands the most hours of your day, and thus it's critical that you see your work or study as a dharma and not some external imposition or burden.

Because it is a dharma, you must not accept work that leads to pain or wanton destruction. The expression of your life cannot, for example, be to cause cancer, steal public funds, destroy the economy, cheat people out of their money, kill innocent animals, or destroy the planet. There can be no happiness in these, and no argument should convince you of the need to accept such a miserable occupation.

To see your work as dharma means to apply the same principle of mindfulness to the many actions that encompass it. You should never see your work or study merely as a means to an end. Work should never be about how much money you're going to make, and your studies should never be about just getting a diploma so you can get a job. This kind of thinking will torture you and make your days long and miserable. Instead, each activity should be done as well as you can, with as much of your attention as possible. Your focus should be on the action itself, not your career, salary, or some other future goal.

If you're feeling stressed by your work, that could be a sign that your mind is out of control. Stress is an indicator that you're either hoping for some positive future result or fearing a negative one. Your mind is dragging you into the future and driving you crazy. Bring your focus back to one action at a time. If it's time to sit in a meeting or class, just be there, present, being the best person you can be in that moment. If it's time to prepare a presentation, sales pitch, or paper, just do that – do the best you can do and don't fret about what's next, scroll through your social media, or answer emails. Keep your full attention on one thing at a time.

Your occupational dharma is a testing ground for your personal development and growth in mindfulness. The multiple demands of running a business, keeping a job, or getting a degree will test your abilities to keep your mind focused on the here and now, on doing what's needed with your full presence and attention. You will constantly be tested in your ability to distinguish between planning and fantasizing. When you get it, though, you'll love it. There comes a beautiful moment when you finally discern the difference between trying to get a sale because of the bonus and trying to get a sale because that's the expression of who you are at that point in time. The difference is from doing your best because you think you'll get some future reward, to doing your best because that's how you can maximize your existence here and now. When you're doing it for some future reward, you will not be fully present, and you'll experience anxiety throughout, anger if it fails, and frustration if it stalls or is less than expected. When you're doing your best as an expression of your dharma, of who you are, you feel great from start to finish, you're fully present in the action, and you take whatever the outcome is in stride.

Overworking?

A word of caution: Occupation dharmas are very alluring, and it's far too common to see people disproportionally give attention to this dharma to the others' detriment. The list here includes seven categories of dharma, but we only have twenty-four hours in a day. It's important to balance them out properly – not too much of one or too little of another. Because people are driven by future desires, and because work offers the most coveted of these illusory future rewards – money – people fall prey to the mistake of spending too much of their time in work. We have discussed how this mentality is illusory and does not translate into happiness, and this certainly applies to the false idea that status and money will bring you joy. Seeing your work as your dharma should help you better establish the limits of its influence over your life. Society needs to recalibrate its feverish focus on work and direct more attention to other fundamentally important dharmas.

I'm reminded of the 2014 story of Mohamed El-Erian, CEO of PIMCO investment fund. El-Erian led one of the world's largest funds, overseeing US$2 trillion. But he quit his job after his ten-year-old daughter gave him a letter listing twenty-two milestone events of her life that he had missed because of work. The year before he quit, he was paid over US$100 million. After quitting, he took turns with his wife preparing his daughter's breakfast. Despite making a fortune and achieving the pinnacle of prestige in his field, he had been feeling deep dharmic disharmony in his life and was miserable. Intelligently, he addressed the problem and sought the balance he needed to experience joy and peace.

4. Personal Dharma

Every personal relationship creates a dharmic demand. The quality and type of relationship determines how "weighty" the dharmic demand is, how much of your time you have to invest in the relationship, and how responsible you are to uphold your role in the relationship. Mothers and fathers have the biggest demands of all. The dharma of raising children is serious. Pet owners assume parental-like dharma with their animal companions. The dharma of being a son or daughter is second-most important. Very close friends also create dharmic bonds. There are varying degrees of responsibility with other family members, siblings, neighbors, and colleagues.

To see every personal relationship as a dharma, as a sacred duty that helps define who you are, means that you have to move beyond selfishness and laziness. You have to become aware of that relationship and feel what it takes to appreciate and honor it. It also means that you want to be fully present when dealing with that person. If it's the moment of day that calls for you to be exercising your personal dharma with your husband or wife, be fully present, exercising as much connection and love as you can. If it's time to spend time playing and educating your children, be there completely. Get into it. Don't let your mind drag you to thoughts of work. Don't pay heed to your mind telling you it would prefer to be in the gym working out, or peacefully reading a book, over playing in a noisy playground.

Personal dharma is of enormous importance. As we saw with the story of Mr. El-Erian, if you don't give sufficient time and energy to your personal relationships, you are bound to suffer, no matter what other gains you are achieving. You have to have the sensibility to know what each relationship requires of you and be ready to fulfill that responsibility with your full attention, with the best of you.

5. Community Dharma

You are part of a community, a resident of a town and state, and a citizen of a country. This means you have shared benefits and responsibilities. The government is supposed to provide you with roads, street lighting, electricity, water, protection from criminals and foreign invaders, and other services, and in exchange, at very least, you have to pay your taxes and obey the laws. Better yet, you should see your community dharma as a call to make life better for those who live around you. Can you help with ideas or volunteer time? Can you get involved in working for civil rights or better government services? Can you help make your children's school better? We can't all think it's somebody else's problem. Where there is an increase in this tendency, we are more likely to find corrupt politicians and bad government services. So, on one end we should at least be conscientious members of our community, paying our dues and following the rule of law; and at the other end, we should be active participants working for a better society.

6. Universal Dharma

Community dharma has a more immediate focus on the community and country in which you live. But we are all interconnected. Not only do we share a natural connection with those of our species; we also share a connection with all the inhabitants of our planet. This connection defines us, is part of who we are, and thus is part of our overall dharma. I call this our universal dharma. As you evolve, you naturally become more and more attuned to the world around you, more sensitive to what is going on. A spiritually mature person is not indifferent to the destruction of the planet or the suffering of others but takes on the burden of doing his or her part to make the world a better place. This is called compassion.

Some examples of exercising universal dharma are 1) doing your best to be environmentally friendly, 2) being a conscious consumer, 3) doing your part in an emergency, accident, or natural disaster, and 4) seeing if you can help when there is mass suffering among people of other nations.

7. Spiritual Dharma

Last but certainly not least is the category of spiritual dharma. Your spiritual self is the ultimate definition of who you are, your essence. Even if at this point you are not subscribing to the idea of being more than this body, you can still understand spiritual dharma as your duty to become the best possible person, to be completely true to yourself. In time, as you understand that you can perfectly define yourself only when you understand your relationship with God, then as part of your essence, the core definition of yourself, you will cherish this connection, called devotion, as the deepest part of your spiritual dharma. To exercise your spiritual dharma is to seriously assume responsibility to know yourself and improve yourself. It means taking the time to practice the 3T Method every day and always practicing the five avenues of perfection of the 3T Path.

The Dharmic Day

On the 3T Path, your day is a patchwork of dharmas—from one dharma to the next, from the moment you wake up to the moment you lie down to sleep. There are no gaps. A balanced life, by this definition, is a life in which you properly divide your limited time and energy among all your different dharmas. Some dharmas have set demands. For example, you have to be at work for a specified amount of time. You should meditate at least twenty minutes early in the day. You have to take your children to school at a specific time, and you have to give them attention every day. Your body needs a certain amount of sleep and food every day. Other dharmas are more flexible. You have to clean your house, but you can decide when. And some dharmas need not be included in your daily routine, such as recreation and giving attention to your parents, friends, or other family members. You can also perform multiple dharmas at once. For example, you can be commuting to work while you exercise your spiritual dharma of cultivating knowledge with an audiobook, or, if you're not driving, with a print book or e-reader. Another example is how, as you go about your life, you practice both your universal dharma of ecological awareness and your community dharma of following society's laws.

Dharma Shift and Mindfulness

Focusing on your dharma is a great way to check if you're practicing mindfulness—if you're really focused on the here and now. For example, you might be enjoying a bike ride and get a flat tire, or working and get a call that there is a family emergency. The natural tendency is to get disturbed. If that happens, just stop. Take some deep breaths. What just happened is a dharma shift. You were content in your dharma of recreation, riding your bike, and then all of a sudden it changed to the dharma of fixing your bike. You were absorbed in your occupational dharma and then were forced to interrupt it to deal with a personal dharma. Don't be disturbed. Just understand that there was a dharma shift. Get into the new dharma; get your mind on it, here and now. Live the new moment well. Don't resist the flow of life and the ever-changing dharmic demands, which often come unexpectedly.

Before you do anything, make sure it's your dharma to do it. Sometimes you come up with ideas that are better not executed. Other times someone may want to push you into doing something that goes against your dharma. So first check, and if the action in question is not your dharma, be firm enough to say no to yourself or others. If it is, though, get into it, despite some attachment to be doing something else, or any laziness or even fear. If it's your duty, your dharma, just do it with your mind fully into it. Don't allow your mind to torture you. Don't be doing one thing while wishing you were doing something else. If you have to do something, if it's part of your dharma, then really get into it, even if you weren't planning for it or don't feel up to it. The result is that you will feel harmony and peace.

Dharma as a Guide and a Way to Simplify Life

As you develop your sensibility to the dharmic demands of each moment, knowing what to do from one moment to the next becomes as clear and easy as following a highway. As you develop this skill, you'll have the clarity of knowing what's the best thing to do at that moment, and thus the natural determination, born of having no doubts, to put yourself totally into it. This allows you to make the most of each day and each action, absorbed in mindfulness and being the best of yourself.

Dharma will also help you alleviate the stress of multiple demands at work or at home—or even worse, multiple desires. Dharma means one main action at a time. Desires are unlimited, and if you allow it, clients, family members, colleagues, and your boss will dump endless lists of demands on you. But once you become confident in your dharma and prioritize your actions according to it, you'll have the peace of mind of doing one thing at a time, with your mind focused on that one action. It's never your dharma to do more than you can—only to do your best.

If your boss gives you ten hours of work for your eight-hour shift, that's his or her problem, not yours. You should know that if you overwork, you'll find yourself without time for your other dharmas. If your company cannot appreciate a well-balanced and happy worker who is in harmony with him- or herself and who has the ability to put him- or herself totally into every action, then it's probably time to find a better employer. You need not corrupt yourself to suit the corrupted needs of greedy companies.

Focusing on your dharma leads to developing the wonderful quality of simplicity. As you focus more and more on what you have to do, on the expression of your true self, you'll naturally become less and less interested in creating unnecessary demands on your life or in purchasing things you don't really need. You'll want to buy only those things that help you better accomplish your dharma, and no more. Living this paradigm shift of focusing on your dharma, you give less and less attention to whimsical desires and fanciful illusory plans for happiness. Just living your dharma in mindfulness is so satisfying and rewarding, you'll no longer feel the need to look for happiness in buying things you don't need. As you develop a growing sensitivity to your dharma, you'll no longer need to look for something to busy yourself with. You'll know what to do from one moment to the next, and you'll value having as much freedom as possible to exercise your dharmas with your full attention. You'll understand that time is your greatest asset.

The more demands you can drop from your schedule, the more peace you'll experience in focusing on your core dharmas. A smaller home means less maintenance and less cleaning. Fewer clothes means a smaller wardrobe. Biking or using public transport instead of driving means less time taking care of your car. And living near your job means less time commuting. Anything you can do to simplify your life will result in more peace and thus more joy. This simplicity means prioritizing your real self.

The Seven Dharmas and Seven Chakras

These seven categories of dharma correlate with your seven chakras. In the yoga tradition it is said that energy circulates through your body. This circulating energy is called *prana*, which literally means "air." Chakras are the hubs of this flowing energy. You need not concern yourself with this energy flow as a separate endeavor. The more you work on yourself, the more your mind is clear and properly focused and the more you make lifestyle choices based on wisdom and dharma, the healthier you'll be. Being physically and mentally healthy means your energies are flowing nicely and your chakras are balanced. There are seven chakras, which correlate to the seven dharmas:

1. Root Chakra (*muladhara*) – vocation dharma. Your vocation is the root of who you are, forming the basis of your contribution in this life.

2. Sacral Chakra (*svadhisthana*) – natural dharma. This chakra represents your physical well-being, to which your natural dharma is key.

3. Solar Plexus Chakra (*manipura*) – ocupational dharma. This chakra represents your personal power and self-will, with your work as its outward expression.

4. Heart Chakra (*anahata*) – personal dharma. This chakra is associated with love and relationships and thus represents our personal dharma.

5. Throat Chakra (*vishudha*) – community dharma. This chakra is associated with self-expression and communication, with your voice. The basic principle of community life is that each person gets to voice his or her concerns so that the group can agree on rules and goals to live by.

6. Third-Eye Chakra (*ajna*) – universal dharma. This chakra represents wisdom and intuition. Universal dharma represents the behavior of the wise and compassionate, those who can be sensitive to the needs of even those far removed from their own lives.

7. Crown Chakra (*sahasrara*) – spiritual dharma. This chakra is associated with spirituality and thus represents spiritual dharma.

INNER PEACE

Inner Peace

The third avenue of perfection on the 3T Path is inner peace, the ability to create internal harmony and balance through awareness and control of one's emotions, motivations, and desires. The type of emotion you're experiencing affects your inner peace. Negativity and negative emotions such as anger, frustration, depression, shame, and despair prevent you from experiencing inner peace, as do greed, jealousy, lust, and the desire for material gain and recognition. They take you away from the here and now and strengthen your fantasy paradigm.

By carefully cultivating positivity and positive emotions such as empathy, enthusiasm, joy, and gratitude; by desiring growth and well-being; and by being motivated by kindness and wisdom, you can maintain a state of inner peace. Meditation is a key component to attaining and maintaining a state of inner peace and should be practiced on a daily basis as part of the 3T Method.

First Steps

As you practice mindfulness, you become increasingly aware of your mind. And as you become accustomed to observing your mind, you develop an awareness of your emotions, motivations, and desires. When you experience a feeling, be it joy, contentment, anger, or jealousy, you should dig deeper. Why are you feeling it?

Even positive feelings can be based on negative principles. For example, you could be enthused because you just updated your conditional-happiness list and you're feeling a rush of illusory future expectation. In this case, the sooner you interrupt the fantasy and bring your focus back on the here and now, on your dharma, the better.

If an emotion is negative – say anger – then it's certainly worth going deeper. Why are you angry? It may be because something happened to crush your illusion that happiness depends on your external situation. Maybe you thought your happiness depended on everyone treating you nicely and someone decided to be rude to you, or cheat you.

The first step is just being aware. Don't just live the emotion. Observe it, understand it, find out its real cause. Get used to tracking your emotions. Then dig deeper to see what's causing them. Track what's motivating you. Why are you doing this? Why are you saying that? Ideally you should be motivated by dharma, but are you? Or are you acting out of desire for future rewards, falling in the trap of the fantasy paradigm? Or worse, are you acting out of negative emotions, such as anger, jealousy, dishonesty, greed, or lust?

It's an amazing experience to learn more about yourself, to become aware of what is making you tick. Most people are frightened by this prospect. But you need not be. You're not so bad. But how can you be happy if you don't know who you really are? How can you find truth, when you don't want to learn the truth about your own actions and emotions? So don't be lazy, don't be afraid. Look inside and get a grip on your emotions, desires, and motivations.

Removing the Weeds

As you advance, you can assume increasing control. You can become a gardener to the garden of your psychology, trimming out negative and destructive emotions, desires, and motivations. You can encourage the growth of positive thoughts and loving emotions. You can reinforce your focus and appreciation of acting in tune with your true nature, your dharma.

Why should you do this? Because the real you has nothing to do with selfishness, greed, lust, anger, jealously, envy, madness, or fear. They are weeds and bring suffering to you and those around you. You want the real you, and you want to live life as a divine expression of the real you. In the yoga tradition, these weeds are said to be the coverings of the soul. We use the term *anartha nivritti*, "taking the path of turning away from the worthless."

The more self-observant you are, the more you can take care of these unwanted influences before they affect your words and actions – just as a gardener will remove weeds before they kill other desirable plants and take over the garden.

As you experience the joy of reducing or blocking such negative emotions and giving room to your true self, rewarding and positive states of mind will arise and you'll feel more in harmony and at peace.

Taking out the Trash

Once you gain some degree of mastery over your current emotions, desires, and motivations, you can search out old experiences and feelings that are calling for your attention, negatively affecting who you are and how you behave. Life is messy, and we tend to accumulate emotional garbage in our unconscious. Unfortunately, this garbage does not go away on its own. It stays there, festering, deep down inside you. If it's significant enough, it can seriously affect the way you behave. It could affect your relationship with your spouse or children or parents. It could affect your work. Many people have experienced that emotional issues can cause disease. From the point of view of self-realization, if you hold an attachment to an emotional trauma, part of your identity is stuck on that traumatized version of you, and you will not be able to grow.

I've learned that by being truthful to myself and observing my emotions, I can find deep, old emotional issues I need to deal with. These issues leave trails. You may feel some anxiety or other negative feeling whenever you deal with a family member, or in a certain kind of situation. Consider that to be the first clue. Be honest with yourself. It's your own internal space; there is no need to hide anything. Admit to all your faults and shortcomings, but also be brave enough to admit faults and shortcomings in those to whom you have a debt of gratitude, like your parents. Our deep emotional problems are usually with those people who are closest and most important to us—parents, children, spouses, ex-spouses, siblings. Sometimes you may have been the culprit. You may have behaved in a shameful way and need to come to terms with that and possibly make amends. Sometimes you may have been the "victim," and you need to get over that – forgive, forget, and stop feeling like a victim.

There are thousands of therapists and therapies out there that can help you in this process. I recommend that you abandon any stigma you may attach to seeing a mental-health professional. Just as you don't feel embarrassed to go to a doctor when your knee is hurting, you should not think twice about seeking professional counseling to attain better emotional health. There's no shame in seeking professional help.

Usually, all you need to do to deal with buried emotions is uncover them. Shine the light of your consciousness on the issue. Accept that it's there, dig it up, and throw it away. Just being aware of it is usually enough. If you can do that, the emotion loses its power to affect you in secret, in your unconscious. It may still affect you for some time, but since you are aware of its influence, you can consciously compensate for it. So don't be afraid of your shadow. Dig deep, be brave, and take out the trash.

The secret is to recognize the emotion and let it go. You should neither ignore it nor identify with it or attach yourself to it. Life is in constant flux. Things come and go. If you can deal with your emotions like this, you'll stay emotionally healthy.

Neuroscience 101

There have been exciting developments in the field of neuroscience confirming age-old spiritual truths from the yoga tradition. Science has shown the effectiveness and power of meditation, mindfulness, and positive thinking. It's also proving the very basis of the yoga tradition: that you have the power to change your state of consciousness and improve your life.

The term used in neuroscience to address this ability to change is *neuroplasticity*. Basically, it means that your brain can literally change. Scientists use the term *rewire* because the brain can be compared to a complex electronic system, with information flowing from one part to another. Some simple practices, including meditation and mindfulness, can change the "wiring" and the shape of different parts of the brain. Part of the experience of feeling different from adapting these recommended practices is that your brain literally changes. In other words, you can upgrade your brain to have a better life.

The field of yoga has recognized this for thousands of years. Yogis have experienced it and given testimony. Still, it's exciting and encouraging to see hard science proving it. I think that these discoveries in the field of neuroscience will help take the ancient yoga path to a place it deserves in the world, as a powerful and advanced system for well-being and enlightenment. More and more, it will become clear that not practicing these techniques is akin to not brushing your teeth or flossing – an unbecoming lack of personal care that can lead to disastrous results.

The Amygdala and Your Cortex

Neuroscience has identified which part of your brain does what, and knowing this can help you deal with your negative emotions. There's a part of your brain called the cortex. It's that big folded-over gray part on top. Your conscious thinking and planning takes place there. When you reason, you use that part of the brain.

Your brain also has two small almond-shaped parts called the amygdala, your "animal brain." It can help to see it like that: your rational human brain and your non-rational animal brain. Many animals, including fish, have amygdalas.

Your animal brain helps you survive; it's your "fight or flight" response. When you are in danger, your amygdala triggers this response, readying you to either fight off danger or run away from it. Actually, there is also a third automatic response: to freeze. Think of a deer facing headlights. So technically, you have a "fight, flight, or freeze" response. In terms of crude wiring, we have our amygdala to thank for fear. In some bizarre cases of damage to the amygdala, a person can become totally (and impractically) fearless.

When you feel your heart rate speed up, blood pressure rise, and adrenaline being released, that's your amygdala in action, the animal part of your brain getting ready for combat or quick escape. It's sensing serious danger. That's great when there is actually serious danger, say a snake, a car rushing towards you, a vicious dog unleashed or a mugger coming towards you from a dark alley. The problem is that the amygdala fires in all-too-common situations such as a presentation to clients, a meeting with your boss, or a talk with your angry teenage daughter. You don't need an accelerated heart rate, more adrenaline, and more blood pressure for these situations. There is no need for fighting, fleeing, or freezing. So your amygdala is often firing away at the wrong times, for the wrong reasons.

And it gets worse. Your amygdala has the power to override your cortex. You may have experienced this—responded to a threat before you even had the chance to think about it. Again, this is great when there is a life-threatening event and a split-second reaction time can be the difference between life and death. But it's terrible when what's triggering your amygdala are run-of-the-mill events in your workplace or home.

Anxiety and anger can get out of control. When you become irrational due to anxiety and anger, it's your amygdala firing away and overriding your cortex. That's why it's useless for someone to try to reason with you when you're under the influence of strong anger, fear, or anxiety. Your cortex has basically shut off, so they have no one to reason with. In those situations you can't even reason with yourself.

Another fascinating (and potentially debilitating) characteristic of the amygdala is that it has a memory of its own, storing information in a different part of your brain from your regular conscious memories. The amygdala will register a sensation when you have a traumatic or painful experience. That sensation, when it resurfaces, will trigger the amygdala, causing anxiety, increased heart rate and blood pressure, or even a full blown panic attack. Psychologist Catherine Pittman and Author Elizabeth Karle cite a clinical example of a woman who after being raped, would have a strong anxiety attack whenever she smelled the perfume her assailant had used.[2] Another example was that of a Vietnam war vet who after decades away from battle started having strong anxiety attacks in the morning. Later, he discovered that his wife had purchased the same brand of soap he had used in Vietnam. His amygdala was responding to that in anticipation of his morning shower.

Dealing with Anger, Irrational Fear, Worry and Anxiety

Whenever you feel a physiological response to emotions, you should quickly take stock of the situation. If you're not in a fight-or-flight situation or just having fun in an exciting activity, you don't want your heart rate increasing and your adrenaline rising. Dealing with a difficult customer or colleague at work? Not the time to lose control of your cortex and get ready to fight or flee. Exasperated with your child? Not the time to get ready to battle. Waiting for a test result or answer from your client? No use for increased blood pressure.

Do you have anger issues? Ever lost control of your reason and done something in anger that you later regretted? Your amygdala took control of your cortex. That's why you can't believe you did something so stupid. You weren't really in control.

This doesn't mean, however, that you're not responsible or that you can't do anything about it. You can disarm the amygdala bomb before it goes off. As you practice constant observation of your state of mind, be aware of the warning signs that your amygdala is going to take over. As soon as you feel an increased heart rate and blood pressure, hit the brakes.

How do you calm down an amygdala in full swing? Neuroscience shows that two things are especially effective: slow, regular breathing, and relaxing muscles.

Just pause, stop the arguing, stop worrying, maybe even step out of the room for a moment. And breathe – deeply and slowly. Relax your muscles; loosen up. Let your body simmer down and your amygdala know that you're not fighting

---

2 *Catherine M. Pittman and Elizabeth Karle,* Rewire Your Anxious Brain: How to Use the Neuroscience of Fear to End Anxiety, Panic, and Worry*, (New Harbinger, 2015).*

off a lion; you're just dealing with a family or work matter. Get your amygdala out of the equation. And thanks to neuroplasticity, you have the power to rewire your brain, to adjust amygdala response.

You can and should be in full control of your faculties, with balanced heart rate, breathing, and blood pressure at all times outside of the rare event of real physical danger. Breathe and relax your muscles to consciously power down your animal brain. This is the key to overcoming many instances of anger, fear, worry, and anxiety.

A Simple Technique for Becoming Positive

Much can be said for staying positive. Obviously, a positive state of mind is preferable to a negative state of mind. In one you feel happy and enthusiastic; in the other you feel depressed or anxious. But at times it can seem artificial and forced to just "make yourself" positive. It may feel like new-age nonsense.

Well, it turns out that it's not nonsense at all. Positivity is a real and achievable goal, and there is a simple technique that can change the shape of your brain, rewiring it to be more positive: neuroplasticity – your brain literally changes when you change your outlook and behavior.

Here's a simple technique, proven by neuroscience, explained by Dr. Rick Hanson[3]. I have put this into practice myself and have taught it to others with great results.

As you go about your day, you'll likely encounter some good things: a beautiful sunrise, a sense of contentment as you shower, the pleasure of a good night's sleep, an especially nice "good morning," a pleasant aroma from a bakery, or a sweet moment with a friend, spouse, or child. We often take these moments in stride and quickly move on to something else. The trick is to really take them in, to make an extra effort to record them. All it takes is about twenty seconds of contemplation, twenty seconds of letting that positive experience sink in. That term says it all: *sink in.* Let it go deep in your consciousness. Do this as often as you can. The more you do it, the more it becomes natural. These positive moments build up, make you more positive in general, and change the shape of your brain.

This same principle can be applied to any positive experience of security, contentment, acceptance, joy, or peace. The trick is to be more attuned to these feelings and then let them sink in.

By absorbing positive moments, you become more positive. By becoming more positive, you absorb more positive moments. It's a simple, beautiful technique.

---

3 *Rick Hanson,* Hardwiring Happiness: The New Brain Science of Contentment, Calm, and Confidence, *(Harmony, 2013)*

Wanting and Enjoying Are Very Different

Wanting is part of the fantasy paradigm. Yes, there is some pleasure in wanting – a pleasure in the anticipation of future satisfaction. But it's poisonous, and with that pleasure comes suffering. It's like the ignorant pleasure of getting drunk. With it comes a hangover and hours of behaving like a fool, or worse. Wanting takes your mind to the future, leaving you feeling incomplete, unsatisfied, and unhappy. The more intense your wanting, the more you'll be subject to anxiety, fear, and anger. There's a famous wisdom saying that helps put things in perspective: "You're richer not if you have more, but if you want less." The less you want, the more content you are and the more peaceful you'll feel.

Not wanting doesn't mean you don't plan. You can plan and still live in the here and now, focused on your dharma. You can celebrate milestones in the here and now. We're so used to wanting all the time that we sometimes doubt we can live without it. We think life will be empty if we're not always full of desires for the future. It's like we've become addicted to a cheap but ultimately painful pleasure. But when we gradually change our paradigm from fantasy to the reality of life, we can discover the real pleasure of enjoying life right now – a pleasure that comes with no ill side effects.

Using the technique of letting good moments sink in, you can learn to enjoy life right now. The simplest acts, such as having a snack or looking at a beautiful blue sky, can become the source of mindful pleasure. You can take this deeper and deeper, experiencing profound joy with common daily experiences and with the realization of your dharma. In fact, the goal of this path is to have communion with the divine at every moment, experiencing increasing bliss.

Instead of wanting, bring your focus to the present and find joy here and now as much as you can, as many times a day as you can. Gradually your mind – and your brain – will change.

KEY CONCEPT OF THE 3T PATH
Beyond Victimhood; Taking Control

Understand that you're in control and that feeling like a victim will disempower you. Your entire well-being rests exclusively on you. It's all in your hands. You have the power to be happy or to be miserable. You depend on no one else and nothing else. When you become more advanced, you will appreciate how God is always helping you and that everything and everyone ultimately depends on Him. But aside from this mystical and sweet fact of life, it's crucial to understand and to live by the concept that you're in power.

On a practical level, sure, use the word victim. If somebody mugs you and you go to the police, they will identify you as the victim of the crime. If a hurricane destroys your house, you call your insurance company and identify yourself as a victim of a natural disaster. We have to take practical measures. That's part of our dharma.

But that's as far as it goes. You have to go beyond victimhood. A victim is powerless. The term victimhood is used to describe a person who absorbs this feeling of being a victim, and thus declares themself powerless and helpless. Victims feel depressed and sad. Some take the feeling so deeply that they lose the will to live. Feeling like a victim will never help you. It's just a path to inaction and unhappiness. As Krishna says in the Bhagavad-gita, "A yogi never laments."

Instead, you should understand that whatever has happened to you is life. It's reality calling. Just deal with it as the new flux life is bringing you. See it all as part of your experience in growth and strength. Perhaps it brings a new set of challenges, new shifts in your dharma. But the focus is exactly the same: you being here and now, focused on your dharma, recognizing your emotions and letting them go. No matter what has happened to you, the joys of life are still all around you. Life is still a miracle, and your experience of it can still be divine.

Focus on what you're doing. That's what you have control over. It's what is really important, what will determine if you're happy or not. It's never about what happens to you; it's about how you respond to it, how you deal with it. Bring the attention to yourself, for it is only yourself that you have power to control, only yourself that you have to improve.

If you accept that everything that happens to you is 100 percent your res-

ponsibility, then you have 100 percent power to change how it affects you. And the inverse is also true. If you feel you have no responsibility, then you have no power. Be a yogi or be a victim — that's your choice.

Of course, we should feel sympathy — or even better, empathy — with those who suffer tragedy. Feel their pain and see how you can help. That's part of the universal dharma. But for yourself, you must not lament. You should give time for your wounds to heal, recognize whatever loss you experienced, respect that . . . and then let it go and move on.

If you feel your mind dragging you toward the past in lamentation, feeling sorry for yourself for something that's happened, stop and bring it back to the here and now. Breathe deep, focus your mind on a sensation you're experiencing now or on doing your dharma. Absorb yourself again in life, in reality, in what is happening right now, and experience the joy and divine beauty of it.

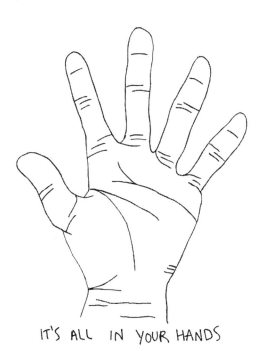

IT'S ALL IN YOUR HANDS

Gratitude

The greatest virtue you can express is gratitude. It's a powerful catalyst of positive change. The spirit of thankfulness blesses you with the ability to see the best of everything and as a consequence fills you with contentment and joy. It's a powerful tool for making your life better. The power of gratitude is recognized by ancient wisdom and proved by modern science.

Melody Beattie, author of several self-help books, sums it up nicely: "Gratitude unlocks the fullness of life. It turns what we have into enough, and more. It turns denial into acceptance, chaos to order, confusion to clarity. It can turn a meal into a feast, a house into a home, a stranger into a friend."

Robert Emmons, PhD, one of the foremost authorities in the study of the effects of gratitude, reports that people who practice gratitude experience benefits in three areas:

Physical:

1. Stronger immune system
2. Fewer aches and pains
3. Lower blood pressure
4. Greater desire and ability to exercise
5. Better care of health
6. Longer, more refreshing sleep

Psychological:

1. Higher levels of positive emotions
2. More alert, alive, and awake
3. More joy and pleasure
4. More optimism and happiness

Social:

1. More helpful, generous, and compassionate
2. More forgiving
3. More outgoing
4. Less lonely and isolated

Other studies show that grateful people also overcome trauma more easily, are less aggressive, are more empathic, and have higher self-esteem.

How do you cultivate gratitude? One simple technique is to write down, be it once a day or as little as five times a week, something for which you are grateful.

Writing it down makes you think about gratitude and look for reasons to be grateful. I like to cultivate a grateful mindset by appreciating wonderful things in life and letting them sink in. As you recognize the good things in your life, you can be positive and enjoy them and also take a step further and be grateful for them.

Another trick I use and recommend is to convert pride to gratitude. Pride can be an obstacle because it strengthens the illusion that your happiness is dependent on external factors and on feeling superior to others. Pride prevents you from learning and from admitting your mistakes or asking for help. So whenever you feel proud of something, be it your appearance, your bank account, your car, your children, your city or country, or something you have accomplished, experience gratitude. Think how blessed and fortunate you are to have these things. And if you feel the tendency to think you deserve them because of your hard work, remember to feel grateful for that hard work, for that fact that you can work hard. Feel grateful that you have been given so many gifts and abilities to do your work, including your health, your coworkers or employees, the government, the market place, the Internet, inspiration, and all the things that contribute to your success.

When you achieve the highest levels of understanding and practice of the 3T Path and realize that ultimately everything comes from God, you will naturally feel gratitude for everything in your life, knowing that everything, including life itself, is a divine blessing. This all-encompassing sense of gratitude invokes profound inner peace.

Jnana - Knowledge and Wisdom

Jnana means "knowledge," but it can also be defined as "wisdom." The traditional path of yoga focuses on the importance of knowledge for our upliftment. The idea is simple: when we do something wrong, it's because we don't know better. If we know better, we live better. Additionally, it's a call to activate our intelligence and emphasize how a life led by intelligence rather than by confused sentiments or base desires can bring increasing joy and spiritual evolution. Wisdom is also just good sense, acting and thinking based on sound knowledge. Knowledge that you don't apply can't help you much; thus the term *wisdom*.

The basic idea is to feed your intelligence with key facts that allow you to make better choices. The goal is to develop the habit of relying on your intelligence, to think clearly so that you can act and react with wisdom in your day-to-day life.

Mental Map

When you're in an unknown place, a map can be essential. By studying it, you can understand where you are, where you came from, how to get to where you want to go, and what possible routes you can take to get there. By seeing where you are on the map, you may feel happiness, knowing that you're near something you need, like a gas station or a store, or you may become disheartened, seeing that you were going in the wrong direction and that it will take a long time to get to your destination. In this way, we have practical experience of how a simple map can affect our well-being, plans, and level of enthusiasm.

We also have another map, always activated and much more complex: our mental map. Your mental map is your vision of life. It shows you where you are, but from an existential point of view. It shows your possible destinations (both immediate and long term), the routes you can take to get there, the routes you've taken to get to where you are, and a general overview of life. This mental map has many dimensions—practical, financial, emotional, physical, spiritual—and directs your well-being. According to your mental map, you'll feel enthusiasm or depression, fear or joy, peace or anxiety. These feelings arise according to the mental map you have. In other words, your life experience reflects your vision of life, not external reality.

But what happens when your map is wrong? If you make use of a wrong map, you get lost and frustrated. If you do not have the correct interpretation of life, your mental map can become distorted. A distorted mental map might lead you to think that there is no hope in life, no way forward, no future. Or it can show that you are stuck on a path without joy or satisfying options. One may think that this is the way life has to be, not knowing that the problem is not with life, not with the external facts, but with one's mental map of the situation.

What do we need for a good mental map? Knowledge. Knowledge can fill in your mental map with information and options you might not previously have known. It can show you that routes you once thought were good are actually bad and won't take you where you want to go. It can show you dimensions of which you weren't aware. With the right knowledge, you can develop a new vision of reality, a new mental map, and with that, a different experience of life.

This is what happened to Arjuna when he heard Krishna's explanations in the Bhagavad-gita. With knowledge, without a single fact of external reality having changed, he went from a having a panic attack, from feeling utterly hopeless, to an enlightened state of bliss and enthusiasm. Krishna corrected Arjuna's mental map.

That is why the cultivation of knowledge, this avenue of perfection of jnana, is so powerful and important.

Get Philosophical

When someone mentions philosophy, you may think, "Boring – that's the last thing I need!" But that may be because you think of philosophy as memorizing which Greek philosopher said what or reading a dense text by Nietzsche, Hegel, or Sartre.

But I'm not talking about studying the teachings of famous philosophers, though that certainly can be helpful. I'm talking about thinking philosophically.

This means thinking properly, using your intelligence. And that entails thinking without prejudice, with an open mind, questioning what you might normally take for granted. It also involves forming logical arguments to explain your conclusions or your critique of someone else's conclusions.

This is also called critical thinking. You can start by asking the following questions about any statement: "Is it really true?" "Who is saying it?" "What is their motive?" "Is there another explanation that makes more sense?"

A key point is to question the authority behind any statement. For example, a PhD in biology or physics does not qualify someone to speak on God. If a person has not properly studied and practiced spirituality or investigated the existence of the soul and God, he or she is not qualified to make claims about spirituality or confirm or deny spiritual truths, just as a non-physicist is not qualified to present, confirm or deny the theories and discoveries of physics, or as someone without medical training is not qualified to diagnose an illness. Before you can deny or confirm any statement, you should first seek to understand the subject matter at hand.

When you develop critical thinking you become free to reexamine and question the values transmitted to you by society, the school system, and even your family. You don't have to reject everything, but you should evaluate it for yourself and not just accept it out of convenience or social pressure.

We live in a world controlled by "spin doctors," people who are paid to convince you that what their clients are saying is true. Others try to fool you for political or religious reasons. So be smart, look deeper, and think hard. When you think critically, it's less likely that anyone will be able to fool or manipulate you. You'll also develop the ability to discover new ways of understanding life. This ability to change gives you the power to develop yourself and attain ever-higher states of mind and progressively more joy.

The Need for Metaphysics

Metaphysical is a fancy word for describing things that are not physical. Practically everyone puts great value in non-physical, metaphysical, things such as love, justice, freedom, and equality. Freedom is not physical. You can't weigh it or put it under a microscope. Yet it's as real as trees and rivers. It's practically inconceivable to imagine life without justice, love, freedom, or equality. You may be so unfortunate as to live life without them, but they are still real. People have gone to war, been willing to die and sacrifice everything they have, for these non-physical "things."

It is thus naïve to expect to understand life based on only empirical evidence. We need metaphysics to explore aspects of life that are not subject to laboratory studies or clinical trials. We need them for a philosophy of life that incorporates the entirety of our human experience, beginning with the experience of consciousness itself. Such a system of knowledge must satisfy reason, be compatible with the experience of life, and be internally consistent.

The combination of modern science and the spiritual science of the ancient yoga tradition results in a complete, fully rational, and internally consistent explanation of life. Modern science doesn't have the tools to study the soul, God, karma, or reincarnation, but the yoga tradition does. The yoga tradition does not bring detailed information about physical nature, but modern science does. The two are perfectly compatible, and both are necessary to understand life. Physics and metaphysics go hand in hand.

Jnana-yoga

The term *jnana-yoga* means "the yoga of knowledge." You'll also find in the *Bhagavad-gita* the term *buddhi-yoga*, "the yoga of intelligence" – using your intelligence to elevate your consciousness. One of the key components of the 3T Method is the cultivation of spiritual knowledge and wisdom.

The yoga tradition brings us metaphysical facts of life that we cannot discover by observing the world, thinking hard about it, or conducting empirical research. Once we take in these facts, life makes more sense. You can explain life with these facts better than you can without them. The explanations are perfectly rational. They make sense and are internally consistent. And nothing in life, or in modern science, contradicts them.

The Source

The source of these metaphysical facts are the *Vedas*. The *Vedas* are a large body of sacred texts covering topics as diverse as health, music, grammar, and spirituality. Yoga is the spiritual science of the *Vedas*, the part dedicated to attaining self-realization. Among the famous Vedic texts on spirituality are the *Bhagavad-gita*, the *Vedanta Sutras*, and the *Yoga Sutras*. There is also a class of texts called the *Puranas*, the histories, where we find a wealth of information on the soul, God, how to live life well, and how different sages attained illumination. The most famous and most important purana is *Srimad-Bhagavatam*. Another important class of texts is the *Upanishads*, which also contain spiritual teachings. In the "Cultivating Transcendental Knowledge" part of the 3T Method, at the back of this book, you'll find a reading list to give you direct access to these fascinating and important sacred texts.

The Soul: Atma

The first spiritual teaching in yoga is that you are an eternal person and not your body. The term *atma* is often used, though there are other words used to refer to the soul. You are unborn, primordial, indestructible, and eternal. You have always existed, and you always will exist. You may have heard this before, but it's worth repeating: You don't have a soul; you *are* a soul. You have a body.

The real you is not made of the same stuff as the universe. You are made of something entirely different. Some people call this *spirit*; I prefer the term *transcendental energy*. The technical term in yoga philosophy is *brahman*.

Consciousness is a manifestation of the real you, the soul. Matter cannot have consciousness. It can, however, be the instrument of consciousness. For example, your TV screen does not contain films and TV shows, but it displays them. If you break your TV screen, you can no longer see the films and TV shows, but they still exist. If you stain your screen with red dye, your films and TV shows will appear to have a red tint, but in reality they have not been affected. Every human, animal, and plant body is a machine made of matter that allows the non-material entity, the soul, to express itself. Different machines affect the display of the soul differently, thus showing different displays of consciousness.

Life is the symptom of the soul. Where there is life, there is a soul.

You are an eternal individual – individual in the sense that you are eternally you. You will never cease to be you; nor will you merge with other souls. You will not merge with God and thus no longer exist as an individual. Though every soul is the same in the sense of being made of the same divine essence, every soul is also different, each existing as an individual. Just like we can say that we are all humans and thus are all the same, we are also all different, each one of us is an individual.

The experience you have right now of being an individual is an eternal reality. You are an eternal person. By "person," I refer to our ability to desire, think, experience emotion, and make choices. Matter cannot do these things. Matter has no desire, no thoughts, and no emotions; it makes no choices. This is the stuff of the soul. Even the simplest organisms want to multiply and survive, even if only by searching out light or heat. The more sophisticated the body, the more the soul can express itself, just as the better the TV screen, the better we can see the film or show. The simplest organisms are like films shown on a black-and-white one-pixel screen. A human body is like a film viewed on a 4K screen with 8.3 million pixels. Vastly different outcomes due to different screens, even if the films are similar. In other words, even though all living entities are persons, this is easier to spot in more advanced species than it is in other less sophisticated bodies.

If I'm Divine, How Come I Don't Feel Divine?

Because you are a divine soul inside a material body, you can choose what kind of experience you'll have: divine or material. The nature of matter is to be dull. Matter is not alive. The more you identify with your material body, the more material your experience will be and the more you'll experience dullness and a lack of joy. The more you value your transcendental self, the more divine life becomes, even while you're inside a material body. Another way of putting it is that the more you live like a soul and not a body, the more you will experience transcendence. Living like a soul means putting into practice what's being presented in this book: living in the here and now, being fully aware of your consciousness, focusing on being alive, living your true nature and essence, and on acting and experiencing life, as opposed to being lost in lamentation and hankering for some alternative configuration of external things. To use the language of the 3T Path: to change your paradigm from fantasy to reality.

The Subtle Body

Souls enter material bodies, inhabit them, and then leave. When a soul enters a body, we call it conception. When a soul leaves a material body, we call it death. But for the soul, there is no birth or death; it is eternal. When trapped in a material body, the soul forgets its true nature. Its consciousness is covered, and it identifies with the body.

The soul is actually covered by two layers of matter. The outer layer is the material body. This is the body you can see and touch, the one studied by medicine and biology. But there is another inner layer: the subtle body. This layer is composed of a matter so subtle that it would not normally register on someone's senses or even more sensitive laboratory equipment. The subtle body carries the soul after death, until it reaches its new body. The soul is never exposed here in the material world. It's always contained by at least the subtle body, and normally by both the subtle body and the visible biological body.

When a soul restarts another life cycle by entering a new body in the moment of conception, its subtle body adjusts and the thinking and emotional processes of the soul become compatible with the new body. A soul in a monkey's body has monkey consciousness, but when it enters a dog's body after death and rebirth, it assumes the consciousness and identity of a dog. That soul upon its death may enter a cow's body, and its subtle body will immediately adjust its consciousness to that of a cow. The body is totally different. The subtle body is adjusted. The soul is unchanged.

Ghosts are the subtle bodies of the dead, usually humans. When a human dies and isn't ready for it, maybe due to attachment, anger, or a desire for revenge, its willpower delays it from moving on to the next birth. It gets stuck between bodies. Because the subtle body is perfectly identified with the biological body, the person maintains the same form as its now dead biological body. When that attachment, anger, or desire for revenge wanes, the hold of that person to its previous incarnation ends, and the forces of nature carry the soul to its next birth.

In Brazil, where I live, there is a religion called Spiritism, with over four million followers. It was originally founded in France in 1850 by Allan Kardec and has as its central practice communion with ghosts. Practitioners receive religious instruction from the ghosts of pious deceased humans and help confused ghosts to overcome their attachments and move on to their next birth. Spiritism was actually a result of the encounter of Christianity with the ancient yoga tradition and its principles of karma and reincarnation.

The Law of Karma

Karma in Sanskrit means "action." The law of karma is thus the law of action. Beyond the Newtonian law of action and reaction governing the physical world, the law of action and reaction also affects the experience of embodied souls. Karma should be understood as one of the laws of nature, acting on the metaphysical plane.

The law of karma is an educational system built into nature, designed to help the embodied soul improve its moral, or dharmic, behavior. Every action you perform has a moral quality to it. Was it the right action? Was it within your dharma to be doing it? If so, did you do it with attention, with care? Did you do your best? If so, then you generated an appropriately positive result. If not, then you get an appropriately negative result. The law of karma puts a mirror in front of you. You get what you give. Or as the Bible says, you reap what you sow.

The reactions produced from our actions come in the form of objects, facts, and situations in life. Everything in your life now – your DNA to your social status, bank account, job situation, neighborhood, planet, health, and everything you own – is the result of your past activities. At every moment, the entire configuration of external reality in your life is a karmic reaction.

The only exception is divine intervention. The more you develop your spirituality, and especially your devotion to God, the more your karma may be adjusted by God to suit your spiritual elevation. It's like getting a presidential or royal pardon. You were tried and found guilty, but the ruling power of the country pardons your crime. Or to give an even better example, if you become a star pupil, then the school may take special interest in your education and adjust your syllabus to help you develop your full capabilities.

Note that the law of karma has nothing to do with devotion to God. One fascinating fact found in the *Bhagavad-gita* is that atheism does not generate any bad karma. There is zero karmic reaction in not loving God. Let's say I have a pot of gold coins. You come to my place and I say, "Please take as

many as you want." If you take the gold, you become richer. If you don't, there is no crime. No one can punish you for not taking it, and there is no moral wrong. Devotion to God is like this. If you take to it, you'll benefit. If you don't, you won't get punished. But you will have missed a golden opportunity.

Krishna explains in the *Bhagavad-gita* that karma is complex. Attempts to simplify it by saying, for example, that if you hit someone in the head, you'll be hit in the head, are just simplifications to help you understand the concept. The system is mind-bogglingly complex, since everything that happens is caused by karma. Everyone deserves exactly everything being done to them. There is perfect justice. In this sense, the law of karma is compared to a perfect cosmic justice system. But like any good justice system, the main objective is education, not revenge or punishment.

Sadly, many people have turned away from God due to not understanding the simple concepts of karma and reincarnation. They blame God for the suffering they see around them. Yet these same people have no difficulty understanding that a wrongdoing must be addressed with a combination of just punishment and education to avoid future wrongdoings. And suffering is precisely that – a combination of just punishment and education to teach the soul to avoid future wrongdoings.

Does this mean we should become callous and lack empathy for other's suffering? Of course not. It's part of our universal dharma to practice compassion and do our part to help diminish suffering around us.

The best way to help diminish suffering is to teach people not to create it in the first place, by emphasizing the benefits of a dharmic life and by teaching them to practice mindfulness. Practically speaking, these two – dharma and mindfulness – are the main focus of the teachings of Buddha.

All suffering is thus within the scope of education – an instrument for creating change. Suffering exists to help you improve the moral quality of your actions and to prod you to investigate your existence. And it works. An enormous number of people have arrived at a deeper understanding of life and spirituality as a result of suffering. But you shouldn't wait for suffering. Delve deep into the mysteries of life and God while the going is good.

Something done in one life may bring effects only hundreds of lives later. Every act creates what is called a karmic seed. Once you understand where you went wrong, however, you need no longer suffer the karma generated by that kind of wrong. The seed is burnt. Comparing karma to an education system, if you prove you have learned the subject matter, you no longer need to take the course. We have an unfathomable number of karmic seeds stored away. Sacred texts tell us that we are like trees. In this life we will generate the seeds to many future lives, just as a tree generates seeds for many future trees.

On this planet, only humans accrue karma. Our free will and sophisticated intelligence give us power. With power comes responsibility. With responsibility comes accountability. Human life is so important and rare and comes with so much power, that in one human life you can generate karma seeds for thousands of lives. Animals, plants, and other beings live out karma accumulated in past human or human-like lives.

Human life is also the only opportunity on this planet to extinguish your karma. As long as the soul remains in the material world, going from one body to another, it will experience the effects of the law of karma. But if you take the lead in your own education, if you take to the path of self-improvement and self-realization, you can, in one human life, achieve the final goal of all karmic education. You can graduate and leave school. To quote the *Bhagavad-gita*, by cultivating knowledge (jnana) you can reduce your karma to ashes.

The law of karma is another example of how this metaphysical knowledge of the yoga tradition helps you to better understand the experience of life and to live better. A rational explanation for all suffering brings relief to any thoughtful person. And seeing every event in your life as justly deserved and an opportunity for growth gives you great power to overcome obstacles and abandon lamentation. The law of karma ultimately confers upon you 100 percent control over your life. You are the sole architect of your destiny. No one other living being in the universe has power over you. No one can do anything to you that you yourself have not brought upon yourself. Others are just external agents of your own deeds. You have the power to choose what kind of life you want to live.

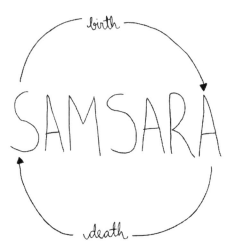

Samsara: The Cycle of Birth and Death and the Process of Reincarnation

After death, the soul reincarnates in another body. This is often described as the cycle of birth and death – in Sanskrit, *samsara*. A more poetic term is often used to describe the vastness of the process: the ocean of birth and death.

The basic motor for this continuous push from one body to another is desire – the fantasy paradigm. As the soul desires future situations in which to be happy, it creates a demand for a future in which that could happen. In effect, the soul demands body after body in its futile search for illusory material happiness. Ending the fantasy paradigm not only brings immediate results here and now, as explained in the Mindfulness section, but also lays the groundwork for liberation from reincarnation. In short, you get what you want. If you want to keep trying to adjust your external reality to suit your needs, then that's what you'll get, life after life. If you want to experience the bliss of reality, in divine communion, here and now, then there is no more need to have a material body. You can experience it now, while in this body, and then graduate from karma school and keep doing it without a material body in the transcendental realm.

Life exists all over the universe in millions of different species. You don't just reincarnate on Earth. And you certainly don't just reincarnate as a human. Human life is actually incredibly rare. Just do the math. You may think that seven billion, the current human population of Earth, is a lot, but just inside your body there are trillions (thousands of billions) of bacteria. You hit the jackpot being a human. You should feel immensely grateful and lucky to be in a human body. Why? Because human life is where you can make serious changes in yourself. It's in human life that you can graduate from karma school and enter ever-higher levels of blissful consciousness.

Once a soul enters an animal or even bacterial body, it has to gradually evolve back to a human life. It's an automatic process that will take as long as is necessary according to the karma accumulated by that soul in its previous human or human-like birth.

According to the ancient texts surrounding the yoga tradition, there are other human-like species in the universe – what we would call *aliens*. Some of them have superior physical attributes and powers. Hollywood has made plenty of movies about them, including *Superman* and *Thor*. Those births are achieved by pious but materialistic humans who desire opulence and power and have not yet given up on the fantasy paradigm. After such a birth, the soul again receives a human birth. Krishna in the *Bhagavad-gita* urges Arjuna, the warrior who hears Him explain yoga, not to fall for this temptation, because of its obvious futility. It's better to use your rare human life to become liberated from birth and death entirely.

After a human birth, a soul has four options. First, it can become liberated and never again take birth, by learning to experience the bliss of life beyond matter, since life is by definition the manifestation of the non-material soul. The more we experience the bliss of this existence, by shifting from the fantasy paradigm to the reality paradigm, the happier we become here and now. This process of self-improvement and self-realization continues until the soul no longer requires life in a material body. Second, a soul can accumulate good karma by pious and attentive practice of its dharma and be born in a superior race of human-like beings in some celestial world for a life of material power and sense enjoyment. Upon using up its karmic credit, the soul would again take birth as a human. Third, the soul may take another birth as a human. And fourth, the soul may so poorly use the freedom and power it has as human, maintaining such a beastly mentality, that it needs to go to remedial school in the form of life as an animal.

As previously explained, the soul may get stuck in a ghostly body for some time after a human body, but that doesn't count as a reincarnation. More ominously, sacred texts describe the existence of hell. Not the absurd and hideous concept of eternal hell purported by some, but a hell that is an intense training center for the wickedly disposed. A morality spa. A temporary experience of profound suffering meant to help the soul overcome serious dharmic deviations before continuing its journey of samsara.

How does the principle of reincarnation help you? First, keep in mind that you have been trying, life after life, to find comfort, joy, and stability in the fantasy paradigm, adjusting the external circumstances of your life, and it hasn't worked, just as it hasn't worked in this life so far. No matter where you go, where you incarnate, you'll still have to deal with one problem after another. Even Superman and Thor have troubles. And everyone everywhere in the universe has to deal with birth and death, and most of us with old age and disease too.

Second, you should respect and appreciate life in all its forms. Each and every living being is another soul, just like you. It deserves your respect and care. Life is sacred.

Third, you can appreciate why people are so different. Each one of us has a history during which we have accumulated lessons, fears, and attachments that are particular to us, different from everybody else's, even someone who has shared much of your life experience, such as a sibling or long-term friend or spouse.

Fourth, if you really come to accept this fact as real, as 25 percent of Americans believe it to be, it would be wise to adjust your life plans to include tools and strategies to deal with it, to see what the options are and how to maximize your current rare human life to become free from the cycle of reincarnation. The beauty of the 3T Path is that you can maximize your well-being, have the best life experience you can, and at the same time work toward becoming free of samsara.

Three Levels of Reality: Dreams, the Material World and the Transcendental Realm

The shift beyond samsara requires you to understand the different levels of reality you can access: dreams, the material world, and the transcendental realm.

The material world is what you're experiencing now in the form of your regular day-to-day experience as a soul in a material body. In this reality you experience personhood. You're an individual person with desires and emotions. You make choices and you reason. You experience having a body. You experience a world with an endless variety of forms and colors. You experience contact with other persons and things, which result in different sensations.

Then practically every night you enter another level of reality – a dream world. That world is not made of the same stuff as the material world. The water in your dream is not H2O. It's made of something else. Your body in the dream doesn't have any actual cells. And yet you still experience individual personhood, a variety of forms and colors, interactions with other people and things, and different sensations. And while you're dreaming, you believe in it; that is your reality, life as you know it, as long as the dream lasts. Then you wake up. As you awaken, you may notice two things: 1) you become aware that you were having a dream, and 2) everything seems to be more real. Experiencing a higher level of reality, the waking state, you can understand that you were experiencing a less real, more confused, less luminous reality.

We usually consider only these two levels of reality. But since time immemorial, spiritualists have presented another: the transcendental realm. In some traditions this is called the Kingdom of God. In the yoga tradition it is called Vaikuntha, which literally means "a place without anxiety." This is the final level of reality, reality with a capital R, the real reality. In this reality too you'll experience individual personhood, a variety of forms and colors, interaction with other people and things, and different sensations. The transcendental realm is made of neither the stuff of the material world nor the stuff of dreams. It's made of something else: pure transcendental energy, the same stuff that composes the soul and God.

There are strong parallels between discovering and accessing this reality and waking up from a dream, and many cultures say that to become self-realized is to "awaken." Once you experience transcendence, even a glimpse of it, you understand that you were previously experiencing a lesser form of reality and that you were having a more confusing and less real experience of life.

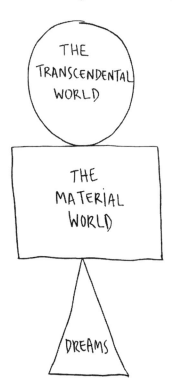

The yoga tradition offers the means for shifting your existence from the material world to the transcendental realm. Since you are a soul made of transcendental energy, that's where you belong. That's where you can experience life to its fullest and most blissful extent.

Samadhi, Moksha and Prema

The state of being fully awakened and totally focused on the transcendental realm is known as *samadhi*, the final state of yoga. Samadhi is achieved while in the material body, almost always a human body. It is described by Krishna as conferring "unlimited happiness," even when the yogi is surrounded by adversities. It's a state of absolute peace, where nothing more affects your well-being. In samadhi you achieve nirvana, which means "blowing out," extinguishing anything that was causing a disturbance in your consciousness, ending all suffering. In this state you achieve a placid blissful mind. As a result of your efforts, you'll also experience higher and higher states of well-being and peace. It is the highest, greatest goal.

Once samadhi is achieved, the soul has no more need to reincarnate. This is moksha, liberation from birth and death, graduation from the school of karma. The soul continues its activities in the transcendental realm.

Above even moksha is prema: love of God. As the soul becomes free from identification with matter, its natural qualities come to the surface. Of all its abilities, topmost is the ability to love – loving is the fullest expression of our essence. To love purely requires freedom from the impurities of ignorance, selfishness, anger, greed, lust, jealousy, madness, and envy. Another way to describe the process of self-improvement and self-realization is that you work on ridding yourself of the coverings of ignorance, selfishness, etc.

Love also requires an object of love. You love someone. But here in the material world, everyone is trapped inside a material body, covered by these impurities. So despite your attempts to love your children, parents, spouse, and friends, there are limits, which is why you sometimes experience frustration and dissatisfaction. To maximize your ability to love, you need to find a perfectly lovable person free of any such impurities. Once you do that, the challenge is to work on your own limitations, because in a relationship with a perfect person, you can experience perfect reciprocity. As you love, you'll feel perfectly loved.

That perfect person is God – an infinitely attractive person who possesses all positive attributes and qualities to an infinite degree. *Krishna* means "the all-attractive." As you advance to perfection, you can experience the bliss of perfectly loving an endlessly lovable Supreme Person.

Special Note to the Reader: From this point on I'll be presenting information on God and then devotion to God. As I mentioned in the introduction, I empathize with those who aren't open to this subject matter, because I was like that myself. If you don't think you're ready for this, skip to the Lifestyle Choices of the 3T Path section and take it from there. You can always come back to this later, when you feel you're ready.

God

Three Aspects of God

There are three aspects of God described in the yoga tradition: Brahman, Paramatma, and Bhagavan.

Brahman refers to the total transcendental energy and also to God as energy. Some use the term *light*. Brahman has no features, no form, no personality. You can think of it as God's aura. You have energy radiating from you. If someone places his or her hand near your body, he or she will feel heat. Some people claim to see or feel auras, others to take pictures of them. The energy or aura we radiate only goes so far. With God, because He is infinite, it pervades everything.

But the concept is the same: it's a formless, featureless energy. But you can feel it and experience it, and it is divine.

Paramatma means "super soul." It is the aspect of God in each and every living being, and in each and every minute aspect of nature (even down to subatomic particles). Because of God's infinite nature, He can be fully present simultaneously in an infinite number of places. Paramatma is God fully present at the side of every soul in every living body and in every particle of matter. Since Paramatma is a form of God, it has features. Dhyana-yogis, adepts in the yoga of meditation, were trained specifically to meditate on the form of Paramatma in their hearts, described as having four arms and lotus eyes, holding symbolic objects in His hands, and wearing jewels and beautiful clothing. But with Paramatma there is little emphasis on personality, on loving exchanges. It's a more static form of God, similar to the deities you'll find in temples. Your body is literally a temple of God.

Lastly there is Bhagavan, the complete and personal aspect of God – God with all His full features, displaying His personality, in action, always surrounded by His loving associates, and in His abode in the transcendental realm. Again, because God is infinite, He can manifest unlimited numbers of complete Bhagavan forms simultaneously, displaying different features and different personal traits and appearing in different abodes with different associates. This is His divine opulence.

All three of these aspects are forms of God, and to relate to any of them makes you a yogi. Clearly, though, it's most rewarding to relate to God personally, as Bhagavan. And though technically the form in your heart is Paramatma, you can relate directly to Bhagavan here and now. Think of it as transcendental call forwarding. Since God is one, despite His different aspects, the Paramatma aspect of God in your heart can connect you to His Bhagavan aspect, just as His general presence throughout existence as Brahman can also connect you to His Bhagavan aspect. You'll experience an endlessly rewarding loving relationship with the Bhagavan aspect of God, which has brought limitless joy to billions of people.

Impersonalism vs. Personalism

Those who accept the existence of God fall into two categories: those who believe that God's ultimate aspect is personal and those who believe it is impersonal, or to use the language of the yoga tradition, those who think God is only Brahman and those who have communion with God as Bhagavan: impersonalism and personalism. Throughout history the personalists have far outnumbered the impersonalists, be it in the Christian, Jewish, Islamic, Buddhist, or yoga tradition.

It is understandable that people are sometimes put off by God. He has been slandered and misrepresented. He has been portrayed as genocidal, sexist, racist, jealous, homophobic, and violent. In His name people have killed and tortured, cities of innocent men, women, and children have been destroyed. In His name, acts of terrorism, murder, and rape are still being carried out. He has been accused of being a religious fanatic, willing to eternally torture any of His children who misinterpret this or that minute theological detail. The very concept of an eternal hell would make God the most evil being imaginable.

Thankfully, this portrayal of God is grossly slanderous and wrong. The groups who promote hatred and violence in the name of God – not God Himself – are the ones who deserve our revulsion.

Still, the West has lived under strange and disturbing portrayals of God for two thousand years, and this has caused a kind of collective post-traumatic stress disorder. A lot of people just don't want to hear anything about God. At the first mention, they duck for cover or run away.

Because God has such a bad reputation in the West, there has been a tendency to introduce the spiritual aspects of the yoga tradition without any reference to Him. Peacefulness, mindfulness, control of the mind, coming to terms with your emotions, living a dharmic life, cultivating gratitude, positivity, seeing the oneness in all – this is all naturally attractive. As a result, the yoga tradition has come to the West in a version that has been stripped of its personal aspects, and this has given traction to more impersonal interpretations of yoga. Buddhism too, which has its roots in impersonal yoga, is non-devotional and totally devoid of the concept of God in its more popular Western presentations.

Most yoga groups are not openly teaching or promoting impersonalism in an obvious way. They simply gloss over God and make little reference to devotion, sometimes hinting at you being God yourself. Few groups specifically promote the concept of there being no personal God or get into any detail concerning the final destination of the soul. In most cases, only a more experienced observer will recognize the impersonalism that is subtly being taught.

Here are some tips for identifying yoga groups or gurus who are promoting impersonalism:

1. They say it doesn't matter whom you worship: Krishna, Jesus, Ganesha, Shiva, or an angel – it's all the same. It's common that in such groups, when you ask for initiation they ask you to choose whom you want to worship.

2. The guru says that he or she is God. Or the disciples say that he or she is God.

3. They prioritize worship of Shiva or Ganesh.

4. They mostly worship the guru. His or her picture is everywhere, including on an altar, and God is not given priority in prayers, on the altar, or in any rituals.

5. They teach you that you are God, instead of saying you are a divine spark of God.

6. They teach that we are all one, without counter-balancing that statement with the explanation that we are also all different, eternal individuals.

7. They say very little about God. When something is said, it's vague, such as "God is love" or "God is light."

8. They say little or nothing about the final state of existence, or end goal to be achieved, or about God's abode.

I have often had students with years of involvement in yoga spirituality coming to my yoga retreat center and being surprised to hear that they were following an impersonalist path. They say, "No one explained these things to me." They usually "kind of thought" they are worshiping God and have not consciously decided not to worship God or to think that they are God. People get initiated by gurus, dedicate years of their life to practices passed on by these groups, and never address the question of God's nature. They usually remain in an intermediate zone, between personalism and impersonalism, not really giving the subject of God the hard thought and analysis it deserves.

The subject deserves hard thought and analysis because it really matters – it makes a big difference. It's not something you can be vague about if you want to be serious about self-realization.

Impersonalism is saying that you're not an individual, not even really a person; you're just Brahman, transcendental light. That's why you are God, because, according to them, God also is not a person and doesn't really exist. Only Brahman exists. Everything is just Brahman.

The consequence of this thinking is that ultimately there is no love, because love is for people. Love means a lover, love, and the object of love. In the impersonalist concept, there are no distinctions. It's all one. No variety. No colors. No flavors. Just Brahman – one transcendental radiance. And your end goal is to understand this and give up your notions about being a person, an individual – having feelings, dancing, kissing, looking at stars – and just fuse with Brahman for eternal radiance.

Impersonalist teachers seldom make this clear, even though, if pressed, it is their philosophy. Instead, they focus on the more immediate benefits of mindfulness, harmony, dharma, emotional cure, social service, and humanitarian work.

Of course, these are all wonderful and indeed are also part of the 3T Path. But my inspiration is to present the complete path, because the benefits of following it are immeasurable. Sometimes people are so happy and impressed with the many wonderful results of just practicing the first three avenues of perfection of the 3T Path – mindfulness, dharma, and inner peace – that they lose interest in getting into the last two: jnana and devotion. Yet traditionally, these last two are the main focus and bestow the greatest benefits of all.

I like being a person. I like variety. I like interacting in a loving way with kind-hearted people. And I find it irrational to have a reality without God, without a source of everything and everyone – an infinitely attractive, infinitely loving and lovable supreme person. Ask yourself if you don't prefer an eternal personal loving existence, with infinite variety and bliss in a divine abode, to just "glowing" as Brahman. For me, it's a no-brainer.

On the purely rational platform personalism makes more sense than impersonalism. Here are several arguments that make the impersonalist concept difficult to accept:

1. *Cause and Effect* – If the material world and life as we see and experience it is the creation of something greater, of God, then we can understand the God's nature by analyzing the creation; we can see the world as the effect and God as the cause. Aspects found in the cause must also be present in the effect. For example, if you wake up and the streets are all wet (the effect), then what caused that to happen must contain water, such as rain (the cause). It would be irrational to point to anything without water as the cause of the streets being wet. Life as we know it is predominated by personality; we can't speak about our life experience without it. Personality is a major, if not the greatest, component to reality as we know it (the effect). Therefore, it's irrational to conclude that there is no personality in the cause (God).

2. *The Life Simulator* – Both personalists and impersonalists in the yoga tradition accept that material reality is illusory. The Sanskrit word for this illusion is *maya*. In the Abrahamic traditions this is not directly spelled out, but the idea is the same: this material world is not the ultimate reality; life in the Kingdom of God is where life really happens. Hridayananda Das Goswami, an American spiritual master with disciples all over the world (including myself), who holds a PhD from Harvard University in Indian and Sanskrit studies, makes a comparison

between flight simulators and our experience in the material world. Life as we experience it here can be an effective illusion, useful in any sense, only if it simulates our real, transcendental, experience of life beyond this material world. "Pilots are trained in flight simulators," he argues. "The simulator is useful only if it simulates real flight. In the same way, the material body, as a simulator of real life, wouldn't have any value if the soul was impersonal or eternally disembodied."

3. *No Person, No Desire, No Creation* – If God were not a person, there could not be any creation, because to create, there must be a desire, a purpose. And desires and purposes are possessed only by persons. There is no logical connection between a complex world of personality, form, and variety and a supreme power that is just radiance. Similarly, if the soul in its pure state is just light, without personality, then it too could not have desired or chosen to experience embodied personal life.

4. *If It's All One, Why Is It Two?* – If it's all Brahman, what is maya? And how can maya overpower Brahman? If ultimately everything is just this undivided transcendental radiance called Brahman, what is this illusory power called maya? If maya is something else, then we no longer have just Brahman. It's at least Brahman and maya. And to complicate matters further, how can this illusory power overcome Brahman (you and me)? If we are God, what power is this that has us fooled for millennia, that has forced us into so much suffering? The answer is that it is God's power of illusion, maya, that can overcome us, because God is greater than us and we are not God. As individual personal souls, we have chosen to come here in the attempt to experience the illusion of the non-existence of God. As soon as we no longer are interested in living this illusion, we no longer remain in maya.

5. *No Love, No Variety, No Activity?* – The conclusion that there is no individuality, no love, no variety, and no activity is counter-intuitive. It goes against everything we value. It's a concept that is as strange as it is disconcerting. It's spiritual suicide. Maybe life isn't perfect now, but to give up on personal existence forever is a disturbing concept.

When pressed with such arguments, impersonalist philosophers attempt to refute them with the classic line "Words cannot describe the truth." Don't fall for this. Impersonalist philosophy has produced libraries full of books, so impersonalists certainly have no qualms about using words to promote their ideas. This reply is simply a statement of logical bankruptcy. Impersonalism doesn't make sense in important ways, and because of this, counter-arguments cannot be refuted.

The yoga tradition presents the personalist viewpoint, which is far more rational, pleasing to the mind, and in harmony with what we value most in life.

The Transcendental Body of Bhagavan

Once you overcome the two hurdles of ignoring God and thinking God is just light or energy (Brahman), you can begin to learn more about the characteristics and nature of God as described in this ancient tradition of the yoga of devotion, bhakti-yoga. From here on, when I say God, I'll be addressing God as Bhagavan, the full personal aspect of God.

For many people, the most difficult concept to accept is God having a form, a body with arms, legs, lips, eyes, and hair. People have three problems with this: 1) the concept is just alien to them, probably because of the Abrahamic culture predominant in the West, 2) they falsely presume that form is limiting, and 3) they think form and bodies are exclusive to the material world.

There are scant descriptions of the form or body of God in the Jewish, Christian, or Islamic traditions. There are general aspects of God's nature as the Lord or as the Creator or Father, but no detailed descriptions. As a result, the very concept of God having a form or not, let alone what that form would be like, is left mostly untouched. These traditions value the Bhagavan aspect of God, as they pray to God and expect Him to "hear" their prayers, speak of God "looking down upon" them and "protecting" them, and understand that there is a "Kingdom of God" and that those who are pious and devoted will be "with God." These all clearly refer to a personal God, not just a transcendental radiance. But there are no resources to deepen this understanding, as the subject is beyond the scope of the Old Testament, New Testament, or Quran.

The almost unconscious cultural reluctance to accept the idea of God having a body fuels the erroneous argument that form is limiting. In fact, the opposite is true – form broadens the possibilities. It is lack of form that is limiting. Language is a good example. It is made possible by using building blocks – letters, words, sentences, and punctuation marks – as well as rules about how to arrange them. If it weren't for these building blocks, our communication would be rudimentary – grunts and scribbles. The more sophisticated one's knowledge is of these forms, the more freedom there is for expression.

Music too is based on form: notes, chords and tempos combined to create the desired effect. Only due to this structured form is music even possible. Without form, we would have only random sounds.

Think of your personal existence. Does being a person make any sense to you without a body with which to express yourself? Can we even speak of a complete personal existence with no mouth to speak, no eyes to see, no ears to hear, no hands to touch, no tongue to taste, no nose to smell? It's absurdly limiting to not have a body.

The argument then shifts to the nature of transcendental energy. If you give it some thought, you can see that form is necessary in the material world and gives greater – not less – freedom. Having a body is necessary for existence as we know it. Sensory deprivation, floating in an isolation tank, might be relaxing for an hour or so, but having truly zero sensory input would drive a person to insanity and death.

Even beyond our body, form is everywhere. Can we even imagine reality without form? Still, never having been exposed to the concept of transcendental reality, form, and activity, people jump to the conclusion that there can be no form beyond matter.

There is no reason to conclude this. In fact, there is plenty of reason not to. First, there is no logical support for the idea. Again, you already experience non-material form every night in dreams. There is nothing about transcendence that requires there to be no form. Second, lack of form and activity makes it impossible for there to be personal existence – or loving interaction. If you reject transcendental form, you're back to the impersonal conception of God, of spirituality being only Brahman, only a transcendental radiance, which is irrational, incomplete, and contrary to the experience of billions of devotees of God in different traditions. It is also contrary to the knowledge of the yoga tradition.

Form can be constituted of something other than the stuff of this universe. But to be more than a limiting impersonal glowing radiance, reality requires form. And among the innumerable forms necessary to create a background for existence, the form of a body is necessary for each person to fully express him- or herself. This applies to even the Supreme Person, God. This combination of each perfected soul having his or her transcendental body interacting in endless loving exchanges with God in His transcendental body in a transcendental abode of unlimited variety and color makes for an infinitely blissful eternal existence.

The Avatar

There are two kinds of avatars: soul avatars and God avatars. In Sanskrit *ava* means "down" and *tar* means "crossing." An avatar is thus that person who has crossed down from the transcendental abode into the material world. Soul avatars show the way to enlightenment with teachings adjusted to the people they've come to help. A God avatar not only teaches the path of spiritual perfection, but simultaneously presents Him- or Herself fully to the souls of the material world. This is how souls in the material world can have specific knowledge of different Bhagavan forms of God.

Soul avatars are perfected souls, souls from the transcendental realm who accepted the mission of coming to the material world for some divine purpose. They are technically called shakti-avesa avatars. *Shakti* means "power," and *avesa* means "part." This indicates that they come with a portion of God's power to accomplish their mission. Two of the most famous examples of such avatars in Western culture are Jesus and Buddha. When a soul avatar comes, he or she must accept a material body, because without one a soul cannot interact with anyone or anything in the material world. Soul avatars usually come alone but by divine arrangement get help from advanced souls already present. Soul avatars do not present new knowledge about God; they emphasize or adjust existing spiritual knowledge.

Jesus, for example, was recognized as a rabbi, a Jewish teacher. His teachings don't stray very far from the Jewish tradition. But he came with such divine power to repackage Judaism's message and emphasize certain key points, that billions of people continue to be enlightened and inspired by his coming.

Buddha, who came about 2,500 years ago, certainly had contact with the yoga tradition, which existed for thousands of years before his appearance. He emphasized dharma, mindfulness, and detachment, all elements of the yoga tradition. To this day, in many branches of Buddhism practitioners are called yogis. Buddha didn't teach anything that wasn't already present in the yoga tradition. But his "portion of God's power" allowed him to emphasize specific teachings and re-present them in a way that was both effective for and useful to humanity, spawning hundreds of spiritual movements and to this day inspiring nearly half a billion people to live a happier, more compassionate life.

God avatars are the direct descent of a Bhagavan form of God to the material world. God never accepts a material body, since the material energy is fully under His control; it's His energy. He doesn't need a material body to manipulate and navigate the material world. He doesn't need a material body to be seen or touched or heard. All this can happen by God's will alone.

Another major distinction of God avatars is that God comes with an entourage of soul avatars and even other God avatars. Some Bhagavan forms of God act, and thus come, together.

Finally, God avatars come for spectacular reasons and accomplish spectacular things. There is nothing discreet about Them. A soul avatar can come and go with only a core group of people recognizing him or her at first (recognition can sometimes take centuries). In contrast, God avatars make Their presence felt and openly establish Their divine power, acting in superhuman ways throughout Their appearance in the material world.

Since God avatars come personally and let themselves be seen, a detailed register of these different Bhagavan forms of God is preserved, with descriptions of Their bodies, teachings, interactions, and abodes. It is the exclusive claim of this most ancient theistic tradition to have registers of God coming in person, being seen, interacting with His devotees, engaging in years of visible activities, and personally teaching about Himself and the spiritual path.

Krishna

The latest such appearance of God was when Krishna descended in 3156 B.C. – over five thousand years ago, centuries before the first pyramid was built in Egypt. Krishna's appearance was all the more special because tradition holds Him to be the highest, most complete Bhagavan form of God. His appearance had all the elements of a God avatar in spectacular fashion.

The reason for Krishna's descent and an elaborate presentation of His teachings can be found in the second book recommended in the 3T Method reading list – *A Comprehensive Study Guide to the Bhagavad-gita with Literal Translation*, written by my spiritual master, H.D. Goswami.

Krishna's core teachings are contained in the *Bhagavad-gita*, the most important text on yoga. Because of the influence of hatha-yoga, the popular form of yoga that focuses on physical postures, some people claim that Shiva is yoga's original teacher. But in the *Bhagavad-gita*, which predates the practice of hatha-yoga by thousands of years, Krishna says that He has come to teach yoga, as its knowledge had been lost. Krishna is the father of yoga, and it's only because of Him that yoga is known to us now. Krishna is also addressed in the *Bhagavad-gita*, as the master of all masters of yoga.

Krishna teaches the complete path of yoga with the end goal of attaining Him, in full consciousness of Him – in attaining "Krishna consciousness." Among the *Bhagavad-gita's* most important teachings are the nature of the soul, how to act without accumulating more karma (karma-yoga), the power of cultivating transcendental knowledge (jnana-yoga), the supremacy of devotion (bhakti-yoga), the qualities of material nature (gunas), how best to live to maximize your spiritual strength and well-being, and the nature of God. In the *Bhagavad-gita's* description of God is the fundamental concept that both material and spiritual energies are His – material nature is also divine – and that everything you experience is a combination of the two. Another fascinating point is that God is time, which could explain why the subject of time and its irreversibility has eluded understanding by physicists.

Krishna came with a large entourage, including several other Bhagavan forms of God, most importantly the highest female aspect of God, Radha. Included in His entourage was also a writer/chronicler avatar, Vyasadeva, in charge of preserving all the major teachings and events of Krishna's life for posterity.

Krishna was present on Earth for 125 years. His life is usually divided into two parts: His childhood in Vrindavan, a cow-herding village surrounded by beautiful forests, rivers, and hills, which lasted 11.5 years, and the rest of His life outside of Vrindavan, first at Mathura for 10.5 years and later in Dvaraka for the remainder of His time on Earth. These three places remain important places of pilgrimage, with Vrindavan being the most important for devotees of Radha and Krishna.

Krishna arrived in a formal, fully clothed, bejeweled four-armed form but then assumed the body of a newborn baby to act out His life amongst humans. From that point on, he played out the development of a human, though once He reached the form of a late teenager he maintained His youthful appearance with no signs of aging until His departure at age 125.

Since God is the source of everything, He possesses all qualities to an infinite degree, which is why He is infinitely attractive. The word *Krishna* in Sanskrit can be translated as "attracting by bliss" or "all-attractive." Krishna's incredible beauty is emphasized more than any other avatar's. He has a dark bluish coloring, locks of dark hair, and a powerful build. It's worth noting that His body is purely transcendental, not made of material energy. This point is repeatedly emphasized both in the *Bhagavad-gita* and in other important sacred texts.

The avatars who come in human-like form act out life as a human to a certain extent. There is an element of dramatization in these appearances, of acting out a role – an element of theater in the sense of a divine script to draw out the most emotion and make the passage of the avatar memorable. Obviously it worked, as here we are talking about it nearly 5,200 years later.

From His earliest moments, Krishna demonstrated this dual identity of being the all-powerful Supreme Lord and simultaneously playing the role of a human. He accomplished this by performing a series of impossible feats even as a baby and young child. His activities are called *lila* (pronounced "leela"). Common among these impressive feats were Krishna's exciting battles to the death with non-earthly, powerful foes sent to kill Him, which occurred throughout His Vrindavan years. Another famous feat was His lifting of a mountain with His left pinky finger when He was only seven, defending all of Vrindavan from the wrath of Indra (the Vedic equivalent of Zeus or Thor).

While these acts established Krishna's divine and heroic powers, the real focus of the tradition is His sweetness. The inhabitants of Vrindavan, already-pure souls who had appeared there to be with Krishna, demonstrated their love by acting out loving exchanges with Him – pure loving hearts directing their focus to an infinitely lovable God. Sweetness, charm, humor, beauty – Krishna demonstrated all these and more to an infinite degree. This is the nature of God, but most especially of Krishna in Vrindavan – an infinite sweetness and intimacy with pure souls who overlooked the fact that He was God and instead loved Him for His personal qualities and infinitely attractive nature.

Krishna was fond of playing His flute. Since God is the source of all musical talent, His playing mesmerized all the residents of Vrindavan. He was also fond of wearing yellow silk clothing, a peacock feather on His head, and a garland made of forest flowers. These transcendental, loving, and intimate exchanges in Vrindavan are the highest focus of devotees in the Krishna tradition, called bhakti-yoga, and remain a major element in the cultural history of India. The most famous of these exchanges, often portrayed in literature, theatre, and the visual arts is Krishna's romantic dance under the full moon with the cowherd maidens of Vrindavan – known as the rasa-lila, the lila of the circular dance.

"I would believe only in a God that knows how to dance," said the German philosopher Friedrich Nietzsche. Nietzsche had the right idea. How disappointing would it be if God turned out to be less interesting than thousands of mere humans on Earth? A God who doesn't dance, play music, and joke or who has no interest in romance? This ancient tradition presents detailed knowledge about a loving, intelligent, friendly, beautiful, charming God who dances; takes care of animals; loves rivers, forests, and hills; and plays the flute.

In Vrindavan, young women swooned at the sight of Krishna; older ones loved Him as a mother loves her child. The other boys loved Krishna as their best friend – some seeing Him as a big brother, some as an equal, and others as younger brother for whom they must care.

Outside of Vrindavan, Krishna assumed the role of a princely warrior and had to battle against a host of evil beings. When not in battle, He played the part of a prince, enjoying palace life and in Dvaraka the role of husband and father with many wives and children. In that culture it was acceptable to have many wives (and even many husbands). For each wife, Krishna created an expansion of Himself, and they each had their own luxurious palace. During His adult life, Krishna's opulent, royal, and heroic qualities were emphasized, and this pervaded the mood of His loving relationships. Many people are more attracted to this kind of opulence and power in God, and Krishna obliged by revealing this aspect of His personality.

When His stay was finished, Krishna literally flew off, back to His transcendental abode beyond the universe. A detailed description of Krishna's life is found in a most important ancient text, the *Bhagavata Purana*, also known as *Srimad-Bhagavatam*. If you practice the 3T Method, found at the back of this book, you will see that the story of Krishna and *Srimad-Bhagavatam* are among the recommended readings.

God's Abode

One purpose of the descent of God is to give us a better understanding of His abodes. It works like an ad for a tourist destination. You see how beautiful the place is, how attractive the people there are, and how much fun they are having, and this makes you want to go there.

You should keep your focus on the here and now, on experiencing your divine connection as you carry on with your dharma, but at the same time you should be aware of reality in the ultimate sense and where you could be. You should know your options.

The descriptions of God's abode give us a better understanding of God and of what life can be like. Krishna's activities over five thousand years ago help in this regard, as do descriptions of God's abode found in other sacred texts of the bhakti tradition.

Goloka Vrindavan, God's "secret garden," is the highest, most rarely accessed abode of God. Krishna recreated many aspects of Goloka Vrindavan when He came to Earth, providing us with images of this most special transcendental region. Imagine a place of the most splendorous natural beauty: pastures with emerald grass, pristine rivers, forests, lakes, and hills and mountains with beautiful waterfalls and enchanting caves. Trees that fulfill wishes. Flowers of all kinds. Birds, deer, monkeys, and honeybees.

In this idyllic landscape, the town of Vrindavan has a simple, intimate village culture focused on cows and on producing butter, yogurt, cheese, and ghee. Vegans need not be disturbed by this description, however; it is not about exploiting cows. Even today, India's culture promotes the concept of the "sacred cow." In Goloka Vrindavan, the bulls and cows are the loving focus of the community, treated like family members. Cows and calves stay together. The bulls pull carts and take part in agricultural work, and they too get great respect. The cows are daily taken out to pasture by the grown-ups, the calves by the children.

God's abode has the special characteristic that nothing is inert matter. This may be hard to conceive, but consider that matter is exclusive to the material world. In God's abode everything is made of Brahman, conscious transcendence. Thus, everything is conscious, and not just conscious, but perfectly conscious: transcendently perfect and fully enlightened. For example, in Goloka Vrindavan, the nature of love may differ, but everything and everyone – stone, grass, cow, bird, or human – loves Krishna completely and consequently loves all other inhabitants as well. Stones melt in ecstasy at hearing Krishna's flute, birds and deer delight and take part in everyone's daily activities; even the rivers and lakes take pleasure in facilitating watersports and refreshing the other inhabitants.

Even harder to conceive, yet essential to understand, is that God's abode is free of the effects of time. Time in the transcendental realm is at the service of the loving exchanges. It only creates the right sensation of change to enhance the loving sentiments. But time does not march ruthlessly, aging and destroying everything and everyone as it does here in the material world. It does not bring staleness or make things dull. In the transcendental realm, everything and everyone is eternally refreshed; everything is novel and exciting. Every day is the best day of your life – the most exciting, most romantic, most fun, or just the most amazing day you've ever had. Everyone lives in perfect harmony being exactly what they want to be and relating to everyone in general, but especially Krishna, with pure unbound love.

Vaikuntha, which literally means "without anxiety," comprises the rest of the transcendental realm – not one place, but innumerable places, each with characteristics to suit the sentiments and inclinations of the devotee, with the particular Bhagavan form of God to which that devotee feels most attracted. In Vaikuntha the mood is more formal. There is more opulence and awe in relation to God than in the intimacy of Goloka Vrindavan. Vaikuntha is closer to the concept of Heaven in the Abrahamic traditions: God as the all-powerful Lord, loved by His devotees in palatial opulence. Jewelry, silk, and gold ornaments abound. God's female counterpart there is Lakshmi, the Goddess of Fortune. Everyone is extraordinarily beautiful, and the inhabitants move about in flying vehicles, singing God's glory and delighting in His presence. Such are the descriptions of God's abodes in the sacred bhakti literature.

God's Name

Religions may seem to all be different, with wildly different claims. Some atheists use this to support their rejection of all spiritual paths. The major religions of the world, however, are remarkably similar. And there is one point that they all hold in common: the importance of God's name, the "holy name".

In the Old Testament, in the Jewish tradition, one of the major events is the construction of the Temple of Solomon (the first known temple of God outside Southeast Asia). In the inner sanctum of the temple was the holy name. The whole structure was, in fact, a temple to the holy name.

Jesus came centuries later. His Sermon on the Mount is considered one of the most important passages of the New Testament. There, the "Lord's Prayer," the only prayer Jesus taught, begins, "Our Father in heaven, hallowed be Your name" in the Mathew version and "Father, hallowed be Your name" in the Luke version.

In the Islamic tradition, images of God, and even of His prophet Muhammad, are strictly forbidden. Inside the mosques, therefore, many of the principal images are of the holy names of God, Allah, in beautiful script.

In this regard, the yoga tradition is no different. If anything, there is an even more intense focus on the importance of the holy name. It is the basis of the mantra tradition, a core aspect of yoga spirituality. A mantra is a sacred combination of holy names, words, or syllables meant to elevate and direct the mind. If you have already started practicing the 3T Method, you know that one of its core practices is mantra meditation, called *japa* in Sanskrit, the process of focusing the mind by chanting a mantra.

The names of God are as powerful as God Himself. In fact, there is no difference between God and His holy name. God's name has the power to cleanse your mistaken identification with matter and connect you with Him, just as being in His personal presence would. Thus, by chanting the name of God, you enter into direct communion with Him, according to the purity and focus of your chanting. This simple means of getting in touch with God brings great blessings and auspiciousness to your life.

Proving the Existence of God

You may have asked, or heard others ask, "Can you prove the existence of God?" Yes, the existence of God can be proven, and there is a process to do so. The proof of God is to experience God, and the process for experiencing God is the process of God-realization found in the instructions given by God Himself. By following these instructions, we can know God. The entire central focus of avatars, including Krishna, is to share and show the path for others to experience God directly. And the set of practices, tools, and knowledge necessary to experience God is called *yoga*.

You can submit inferior things, things under your control, to tests. You can put something under a microscope; you can take it apart, burn it, fuse it. You can collide atoms. You can get volunteers to subject themselves to psychological tests. But what can you do when you're dealing with a far greater power beyond your control?

We can get a clue to this in the modern world. Let's say someone wants to get a degree from Harvard. The person can't just waltz in and demand to be accepted, because in this regard Harvard is a superior power. He or she must submit to Harvard. Bragging or moaning won't help; Harvard won't be swayed. If the person wants to go to Harvard, he or she has to follow the rules laid out by Harvard and be sufficiently qualified according to the standards Harvard has established. In short, you can't challenge Harvard; you must submit to it. By definition, God is supremely powerful, so there can be no other way to know Him except by submitting to Him and following His instructions. By that process you can gradually become qualified to experience God. Avoiding this discipline and just crying out that God does not exist is useless and irrational.

Concluding the Jnana Section

The Vedic tradition presents a description of reality with a transcendental dimension – with souls, God, and transcendental abodes. Its explanation of our nature and of our individual, personal existence shows us how we can live better right now. So, although it includes a complex metaphysical structure, we can at the same time directly experience myriad positive results. Many of these effects can even be demonstrated in clinical studies in the fields of psychology and neuroscience. You don't have to buy in to the whole metaphysical explanation to start putting the suggestions and tools into practice. People are adopting mindfulness, meditation, hatha yoga, healthy living, simplicity, mantra chanting, gratitude, and many other elements explained in the 3T Path and experiencing life-changing results. Uniquely, however, the 3T Path, presents all these elements together.

All the pieces are wonderful on their own, but put together they are far better. The more aspects of the 3T Path you can practice and assimilate, the better your life will become. People tend to sell themselves short by adopting only one aspect or another. By cultivating wisdom, accumulating jnana, you'll be able to understand the importance of putting it all together and will be motivated to do so. It's essential, therefore, to deepen your understanding and strengthen your intelligence by reading the other books recommended in the 3T Method.

Bhakti – Devotion

The final, most important, focus of yoga is to love God. Love is the highest, purest expression of the eternal individual person, the soul. And to love God is the perfection of the ability to love. *Yoga* means "connection," and nothing creates a stronger connection than love. To connect with God in love is called *bhakti-yoga*, or just *bhakti*. It's not surprising that Krishna says in the *Bhagavad-gita* that of all types of yogis, the one who connects with Him in bhakti is the highest of all. In chapter after chapter, Krishna emphasizes that bhakti is the essential and ultimate ingredient for perfection, without which there cannot be full success in yoga. The sage Patanjali also writes in the *Yoga Sutras* that the "perfection of the perfection of yoga" is attained by "isvara pranidhana," to be dedicated to God.

The Key to Success and the Final Objective

Devotion is not only the final objective in yoga, but also the key to success. As the saying goes, love conquers all. With devotion you'll be inspired to push yourself further in your self-improvement and self-realization. With devotion you'll experience increasing bliss in the here and now and you'll more easily exercise your dharma, knowing it to be your means to express your love in action and service. With devotion you'll have more courage to face your inner demons, you'll find the extra strength needed to overcome the really tough challenges in life, and you'll become wiser. And as funny as it may sound, it's with devotion that you can become more devoted.

Other aspects of yoga have a limited scope of utility. For example, it takes some time and energy to understand your dharma and to live by it. But once you've achieved this, it's done. You can't keep getting more dharmic forever. After some time, you can reach a very respectable standard of dharmic behavior. The same applies to inner peace. It takes time, but once you've managed to get a grip on your emotional health and freed yourself of the effect of past traumas, it's no longer an issue or an impediment to a better life. Even jnana has its limitations. There's a lot to learn, a lot of wisdom to acquire, but in time you'll get enough to understand life, make the right choices, set up the right priorities, and act with intelligence; you'll basically know enough. But bhakti has no limit, no bounds. You can love more and more and more, forever. Devotion works while you're here in the material world and continues beautifully even when you reach the transcendental realm. There is no end and no limit to its scope. It's a source of endless and increasing bliss.

The Two-way Path of Love

In the *Bhagavad-gita* Krishna emphasizes that there is a two-way path of love. His basic premise is that He is ready, waiting for you, and has always been. He loves you. He also respects you enough to wait for you to love Him back. As my spiritual master often jokes, God has no inferiority complexes and no lack of loving relationships. He doesn't need to impose Himself on you. He gives you space. He gives you lots of space, actually – whole universes of it. And when you're ready, He'll be there.

Then Krishna explains the benefits – that once you are open to a relationship with Him, He'll start taking a more active part in your life. He presents a simple basis for relationships: reciprocity. If you pretend that He doesn't exist, He'll honor that and pretend to not exist for you. If you hold Him dear to you, He'll act accordingly and show how dear you are to Him.

Since all knowledge comes from Krishna, He promises to those with devotion to give knowledge of how to get closer. He promises to take an active part in the spiritual lives of those who take shelter of Him, to the point of saying that He will arrange their enlightenment. He explains that only those who approach Him can overcome the powerful material energy, since it's His energy; otherwise, they remain baffled by it.

A major theme of the *Bhagavad-gita* is Krishna's loving invitation for us to become devoted to Him and thus allow Him to help us every step of the way, just as a loving father naturally and ardently desires happiness for his children.

Divine Protection

One of the common factors in all God-centered traditions is that as you open your two-way path of love with God, you experience His divine protection. Security is a significant feature of psychological well-being. It is one of our primal needs for happiness. Those who become advanced in devotion gain access to the comfort of security, especially in times of danger. Devotion will not spare you of pain or death. It's still going to hurt when you cut yourself, and you're certainly going to die sooner or later, no matter how devoted you may be. It's impossible to prove whether or not God has intervened in the life of a devotee. God says He does, and there are innumerable claims by the faithful of traditions throughout time of God's intervention. But regardless, the sense of security is undeniably real, and it has real benefits in terms of your well-being and peace.

Ultimately, as a spiritualist, you'll understand that you're not your body. You are a primordial, eternal, and indestructible being beyond matter, so nothing can ever harm you. This knowledge bestows well-being and comfort, even in the face of certain death. A wise person thus prays to God not for protection of one's house, car, money, body, or family, but for protection against the only thing that can really bring on suffering: his or her desires. So even as you may practice asking God for protection in the mundane sense – and there is nothing wrong with that – make sure you remember the real cause of all your suffering: your desire for future material happiness and your uncontrolled and agitated mind.

Mindfulness in Devotion

In the *Bhagavad-gita*, Krishna urges us over and over again to fix our mind and intelligence on Him. This is the goal of yoga. Keeping your intelligence fixed on Krishna means that you think, analyze reality, and make choices based on your jnana, transcendental knowledge and wisdom, taking into consideration your nature as soul, the existence of God, and what would be most pleasing to your true self and God. Keeping your mind fixed on Krishna means just that: you think of Him at every moment. You see Him in everyone and everything. You are always feeling the connection. Perfect yoga is always being connected and always experiencing transcendental love. Your deepest love is awakened.

This does not come cheap; nor is it easily achievable. Krishna hints that it may come only after lifetimes of practice. But He also says that anyone can achieve perfection in *this* lifetime. In the end, it's up to how intensely you desire it and work for it.

The secret is to always try your very best to connect to Krishna here and now, to get deep enough into reality that you find what – or who – is ultimately behind it all: God.

The Five Flavors of Love

In the Krishna bhakti tradition there is a special focus on attaining loving intimacy with Krishna, especially in the mood exhibited in Vrindavan. In the sixteenth century, Rupa Goswami, a great spiritual master of the tradition, developed "rasa theory." *Rasa* means "juice," "taste," "flavor," or "mood." In rasa theory, Rupa Goswami presents five major "flavors of love," five types of loving relationships a soul can develop with God.

The first rasa is shanti-rasa. *Shanti* means "peace." Shanti rasa is the base flavor, the vanilla of love. It's love experienced with some distance, based on just being there in the presence of God. It doesn't need much personal interaction. It's like basking in the sun. No action is required; you just feel that wonderful sunlight. This rasa is said to be experienced by rocks, trees, animals, and rivers in the transcendental realm.

The second rasa is dasya-rasa. *Dasa* means "servant." So dasya-rasa is the love born out of serving God. Service requires more interaction and more action. You may have a negative impression of what it means to serve or to be a servant. Serving out of financial necessity or fear is certainly undesirable. But serving as an expression of love is wonderful. You know that feeling you got when you helped your teacher carry something or set something up? Or that feeling of satisfying a boss you really like and respect with a sale or work well done?

Or of helping an elderly parent to move about or get up? That's dasya-rasa. Out of love, you accept a lower position, that of a servant. You accept that the loved one, as your superior, deserves your service.

The third rasa is sakhya-rasa. *Sakhya* means "friendship." This is the love felt by friends. That intimate feeling of camaraderie, of shared adventures and of being on solid common ground. Sakhya-rasa requires equality – both people on the same level, both equally helping each other, by acting together or just having a good time, playing together, and enjoying each other's company.

The fourth rasa is vatsalya-rasa. *Vatsalya* in general means "affection," but it is used more specifically in the context of the affection a mother or father feels for his or her child. Vatsalya is the love a person has with anyone for whom they feel a parental responsibility – that love for someone who looks up to them, who counts on them for care, guidance and protection. Souls experiencing vatsalya-rasa with God consider that they need to take care of God, look out for Him, protect Him, and even nourish Him. They assume the roles of a father, mother, uncle, aunt, grandmother, grandfather, or just an elder.

The fifth and final rasa – madhurya-rasa – is the most profound and intense. *Madhurya* means "sweetness" and Madhurya-rasa refers to romantic love – that all-encompassing, overpowering, maddening head-over-heels type of love so often described by poets, singers . . . and spiritual masters in the bhakti tradition.

We are all individuals and as such have different types of loving relationships with different people. The same applies to our eternal relationship with God. It's not one size fits all. Different souls relate differently to God. One type of rasa isn't better than another. It's not like you'd want to be a parent to your best friend. And this doesn't refer only to God in the transcendental abode. There are countless other souls there, and they each love one another according to their relationships. I can't conceive of a better description of paradise than a pristine realm of endless variety where the soul can forever experience all flavors of pure love with other perfect souls while cultivating a special relationship with the supremely lovable God.

Bhakti as Love Here and Now

As we have discussed, spirituality should never be about the future. It all starts with focus on the here and now, and that's where our mind should always be. Not only that, but spirituality must include everything happening in your life. Bhakti is no different. At this moment you're not surrounded by perfect souls. You're not perfect either. We are all works in progress. You're trapped in a material body, and to one degree or another you're identifying with your material body and thus are under the influence of selfishness, greed, lust, anger, madness, and envy. Still, you can do your best to practice bhakti right now. There is the obvious manifestation of bhakti as love of God, which we need to work on every day, but there is also the practice of loving others, despite their shortcomings.

Ultimately, it's all about love. To love is to be spiritual, for love is exclusive to the soul. To become spiritual is to awaken your love and to expand it, to get past bodily identification and show love to those who are not from your family, your city, your nation, your social group, your religion, or your political party. To paraphrase Jesus, what's the big deal in loving your friends and family? The real test is to love those who are acting inimically toward you, even those with envy or ill intent. Does this mean hugging and kissing a mugger? No, you defend yourself or run away. But inside, if you want to experience peace, you should not allow hatred or anger to take over your mind. Instead, you can try to feel compassion and love for all. As you go about life, take on this greatest of challenges. Everyone else benefits, and God is pleased. But it's you who will benefit the most.

And while you're trying to be as loving as possible, develop your love for the root of everyone – God. You can try to water a tree by watering each leaf and branch, but ultimately you must water the roots. All leaves and branches will automatically be benefited. If you water only the leaves and branches and not the roots, the tree will wither. Similarly, you should love God first and foremost, for by doing so you benefit everyone else, as He is the root of everyone and everything. Your love for others should be an expansion of your love of God and your love of God your inspiration to love others.

Love Is Service

The great spiritual master A.C. Bhaktivedanta Swami Prabhupada used "devotional service" as a translation of *bhakti* and, actually, the whole path of spirituality. The word love is often misidentified as just a warm fuzzy feeling. But real love results in service. You truly love someone when you are doing something for them. Love requires action. A mother's love is often seen as the greatest form of love, because there is so much service.

Mother Teresa expressed it nicely: "The fruit of faith is love; the fruit of love is service." Saintliness is making the welfare of others our only concern. This is the goal of spirituality – love in action at its most perfect.

Conclusion – Putting It All Together

The five avenues of perfection on the 3T Path are 1) mindfulness, 2) dharma, 3) inner peace, 4) jnana (knowledge), and 5) bhakti (devotion). Practiced together, they

will place you firmly on the path of yoga. You'll experience ongoing powerful transformation. This awakening is sometimes compared to a second birth.
There is so much new learning and growth and so much change for the better
compared to how you lived before. It's all very exciting. As Krishna says in the
Bhagavad-gita, of all the things you can be, being a yogi is the best. And by
following the 3T Path, you'll be a yogi.

The Ultimate Purpose of Life

Having a purpose in life promotes physical and psychological well-being. "[Re-
searchers] found that people who had a weak purpose or no purpose in life
were 2.4 times more likely to develop Alzheimer's disease than people who had
a strong purpose in life. People with a strong purpose have been shown to live
longer, to be less likely to get heart attacks and less likely to get a stroke," says
Dr. Strecher of the University of Michigan[4]. A life without purpose saps your
energy and drives you to sickness and despair. Life becomes literally pointless.
That's no way to live. You need a purpose.

Using success markers as purposes doesn't work. A success marker – money,
a car, a house, a promotion, 100,000 followers on Instagram – is part of the
fantasy paradigm, existential empty calories. It will not enthuse you for the
simple reason that a success marker is not a true gain; it's just a way to push
back the goal line. Being accepted to a university, for instance – is it an end in
and of itself? No – you just want a college degree so you can proceed to goal
two, getting a good job. But is that it? No, you want the job so you can reach
goal three: a good salary and social prestige. Is that it? Again, no. You wanted
those so you could reach goal four: getting married and raising a family. Then
what? Is getting married and having children the ultimate purpose of your
life? That doesn't work either. You will have a life beyond marriage, and your
children will grow up. Then what? Goal five? Retirement? You get the idea.
These goals are not purposes. They don't define your essence or the meaning
of your life.

A purpose is specific to your vocation, the first dharma category. If your vocation is teaching, for instance, your purpose may be "to transform the world
by teaching children to discover their essence and to practice compassion." If
you're into politics and human rights, it might be "to give a voice to the oppres-
sed, fight inequality, and end the suffering caused by bad governance." An en-
trepreneur might say, "to create something that will improve how my customers
live." These are lifelong lasting purposes. A purpose that is true to your essence
will get you out of bed in the morning and fill you with enthusiasm, day after

---

4 Halpert, Julie. 2014. *"Why You Need a Purpose in Life."* Wall Street Journal, *March 30.*

day, year after year, for the rest of your life. There is no retirement when you've found your purpose. It's a joyful task, the quintessential labor of love, even with all the troubles, setbacks, and doubts you'll experience along the way.

It's great to find your purpose in life, but as a yogi you could go even further and ask yourself what is the *ultimate* purpose in life. After all, your vocation is just part of your current karma, who you are for this life only. When you die, whatever goal you have for this life will be finished. As a yogi, you could add an ultimate purpose to your life – something like "to become fully enlightened, achieve unlimited bliss, and meet God face-to-face." Now *that's* a truly spiritual and eternal purpose for the soul.

After all, if you're going to die and everything will be destroyed in due time, what is the ultimate good of any material objective? If you cannot find a purpose that transcends not only your death but everyone's death, which is inevitable, and even the end of the universe, you have not achieved your full potential. So it's essential to go deep and embrace the ultimate purpose of life: self-realization, full awareness of reality, and pure love.

Having an ultimate, transcendental purpose to your life will push you forward, give meaning to your life and focus your determination, help you through dark times, and give you total clarity. You'll know how to establish your priorities, what is useful and what is not, and what success really is.

In case you're wondering, my life's purpose is "to improve the lives of as many people as possible by teaching the 3T Path and to live in full communion with Krishna in intimate loving service." This has been my purpose for over twenty years. It's wonderful having such a clear, transcendent purpose in my life. Not a day goes by that I am not aware of this goal, and almost every day it has been my driving priority and main focus. It has given me great enthusiasm and filled me with joy.

Life as an Offering to God

There are basically two possibilities: 1) God exists and 2) God does not exist.

If God does not exist, the concept of the soul makes little sense. How could there be transcendental individual eternal souls but not a source of these souls? And if there are no souls, then the atheists are right and we're just by-products of chance – walking, thinking matter. After death, there is nothing. Just matter being recycled. Love, justice, freedom, joy – just illusions. Neurons firing in one direction or another.

If you believe this, really believe it, why live? If life has no sense, no purpose, no meaning, why bother? Some people have ended their lives upon reaching this stark conclusion. But it is a deeply mistaken view of life.

If God exists, by definition everything and everyone comes from Him, or to use the yoga terminology, everything and everyone is His energy. Nothing about you, not even your very self, and certainly nothing in your life, would exist if not for God. Therefore, everything and everyone comes from and ultimately still belongs to God. And as a result, you can only feel perfectly satisfied and aligned with your true self when you make your life an offering to God.

Offering is a key component of the yoga tradition. The Sanskrit word is *yajna*, and it is a necessary aspect of love and service. When you are occupied in loving service to a spouse, child, boss, community, or pet, you are offering your time and energy; you're offering a part of your life. This is good, desirable; it means you're acting in love. It's the opposite of being selfish and wasting your time.

But since spouses, children, bosses, communities, pets, and everyone and everything else are intimately related to God, you can make your loving service to anyone or anything – to any noble cause – an offering to God.

Making your life an offering to God does not mean becoming a monk or priest. It means carrying out your dharma and living your life to the fullest – as an offering to God. Krishna makes this simple request in the *Bhagavad-gita*: "Whatever you do, do it as an offering unto Me."

The difference is in your consciousness. To act unaware of God is to not understand the final dimension and purpose of life. To live and make every dharmic act an offering to God is to be fully lucid and completely aware of reality.

And since an offering is a sign of love, by making your life an offering to God, you can doubly experience love: by acting out your dharma with love—taking care of your child, doing your job, and being a citizen of your community, country, and planet—and by understanding and internalizing your loving connection with God (bhakti) in everything you do. This is the perfection of life.

KEY CONCEPT OF THE 3T PATH
Karma-yoga

Karma-yoga is the yoga of action. It's the technique taught by Krishna to live a life in which every action is a springboard for enlightenment. It's essential to get this right, because it's how you can live in yoga. Karma-yoga will make your life truly spiritual, beyond just having some spirituality in your life.

The stakes are high. Either your action generates more karma, be it positive or negative, binding you further in the material world, or your action is karma-free, bringing you closer to your blissful and pure divine state of being. The Yoga Sutras *explain that there is no middle ground. Your action brings you either enlightenment or further entanglement. Karma is mundane action. Karma-yoga is spiritual action. It's that simple.*

For an action to be qualified as karma-yoga, there are three requirements:

1. *Mindfulness: living according to the reality paradigm and not the fantasy paradigm. You are fully present in the moment, in what you're doing, and you're not desiring or fearing the future results of that action. Your mind is here and now.*

2. *Dharma: keeping your action true to your nature. It's the best of you. It's the expression of your being. It's what should be done, and you're doing it with as much love as you can.*

3. *Yoga: doing it as offering to God. You are aware and connected to God while in action. It's your loving service to God.*

The first two items make your action materially perfect. The third makes it transcendental. Doing your best and offering it to God is a simple way to understand spirituality, and the secret to a wonderful life.

This is the technique to stop accumulating karma. You accumulate karma when your acts are motivated by the result. You're asking for a result, so you get it. Unfortunately, it comes with strings attached. You may have thought you could satisfy your hunger by eating a burger. Well, your hunger was satisfied, but with that came all sorts of karmic implications. Did an animal have to die to satisfy your desire? Major karmic debt. What was the environmental impact of your meal? You bought the burger, but who does everything really belong to? If there is a God and He owns everything, you just committed theft by taking something without acknowledging its owner. How was the wheat of the bread bun produced? Were pesticides used? What about the conditions of the workers involved? And on and on.

There are so many karmic implications in even the simplest of acts, but by practicing karma-yoga, you can opt out. First, don't desire the future results; keep your mind on the here and now. Second, act compassionately and wisely, according to dharma, which already entails, among other things, not causing undue pain and suffering, such as killing animals or mistreating people. And lastly, consciously offer the act to the source of everything and everyone. That's how you can be in but not of this world.

Positivity and Gratitude in God

In the inner-peace section, I suggested the simple but powerful technique of practicing positivity by appreciating the many wonderful things in your day-to--day life and then further emphasized the power of gratitude. Once you overcome your reservations in establishing your contact with God and your devotion starts flowing naturally, you can take those practices to the next level, with even more powerful results.

Everything that is happening to you is the best thing that could be happening to you. You need it. It might feel good or it might not, but that's not the goal. You didn't take birth as a human just for fun. You came to learn and grow and reach a more elevated state of joy and bliss – so elevated that it's way beyond the superficial ups and downs of life. That state of consciousness is far superior to what you can feel "just having fun." This elevated state of consciousness, even while you may be going through adversity on the surface, is far superior to a lower state of consciousness when things are going well. Whatever is happening is part of the process of achieving this superior state of existence. Once you get this and get on the program, your experience of life will become much smoother, no matter what you're going through.

This means that at every moment of your life, if you reach deeply enough, so deep that you see everything in relation to God, you can find endless positivity and experience unlimited gratitude. You can start by appreciating the many good things in your life to the point of feeling blessed, and thus grateful to God for granting them to you. Peace, health, beautiful scenery, stars in the sky, following your purpose in life, sunshine, security, experiencing someone's love, a hot shower, being able to love someone, a full belly . . . the list goes on and on. We each have so many blessings to thank God for. Awareness of this generates well-being and positivity.

What about when things go bad? I try to always remember the simple teaching "There is always someone suffering more than you." As soon as I feel myself complaining about something, I call to mind images and suggestions of how far worse things could be. My first response is to be grateful. Then I think, "Instead of complaining or even remembering that things could be worse, what can I do to mitigate the suffering of others?" Gratitude and compassion will guide you out of any negative feelings brought on by experiencing a difficult situation. Whatever happened, you needed it. Tough love from God. It stings, but it's for the best. Just don't get stuck in lamentation; in due time you'll be able to come to terms with it, or even better, see it as a blessing in disguise.

Once you've activated the power of bhakti, being positive and grateful comes naturally – a major component to living a life full of joy.

PART 3
LIFESTYLE CHOICES OF THE 3T PATH

PART 3 – LIFESTYLE CHOICES OF THE 3T PATH

Your ability to practice the five avenues of perfection on the 3T Path – mindfulness, dharma, inner peace, jnana (knowledge), and bhakti (devotion) – is affected by your lifestyle choices. Your body and mind are connected. The things you subject your body to will affect your mind, and the things you subject your mind to will affect your body. Some habits muddy your mind; others clear it. Some foods dull your mind; others sharpen it. Not only can you make your body sicker or healthier according to the lifestyle you choose, but your mind too. And all this impacts the quality of your life experience and your ability to follow the 3T Path.

It's important to note that what follows in this section of the book are recommendations, not prerequisites. If you are not already doing so, you can and should start practicing the 3T Method described in the back of the book. The purpose of this section is to give you more self-improvement tips, ways to make your life better and to feel better as a result, and also to give you the means of maximizing your potential for growth, as well as your ability to practice the 3T Path.

The Gunas – The Modes of Material Nature

In the yoga tradition the recommendations to maximize your potential for growth are practical applications based on the modes of material nature – *gunas* in Sanskrit. They are given great importance in the *Bhagavad-gita* and in the yoga tradition. The three gunas – sattva, rajas, and tamas – are the building blocks for material energy. They are also the ways by which material energy influences your mind, and consequently the quality of your life. They affect every aspect of your life, including your happiness, determination, manner of speech, food choices, mental clarity, ability to discern good from bad and right from wrong, and even what body you will receive if you reincarnate. It's essential, therefore, to cultivate the guna influence in your life. Dr. David Frawley describes each guna in his essay "The Three Gunas: How to Balance Your Consciousness":

1. Sattva is the quality of intelligence, virtue and goodness and creates harmony, balance and stability. It is light (not heavy) and luminous in nature. It possesses an inward and upward motion and brings about the awakening of the soul. Sattva provides happiness and contentment of a lasting nature. It is the principle of clarity, wideness and peace, the force of love that unites all things together.

2. Rajas is the quality of change, activity, and turbulence. It introduces a disequilibrium that upsets an existing balance. Rajas is motivated in its action, ever seeking a goal or an end that gives it power. It possesses outward motion and causes self seeking action that leads to fragmentation and disintegration. While in the short term Rajas is stimulating and provides pleasure, owing to its unbalanced nature it quickly results in pain and suffering. It is the force of passion that causes distress and conflict.

3. Tamas is the quality of dullness, darkness, and inertia and is heavy, veiling or obstructing in its action. It functions as the force of gravity that retards things and holds them in specific limited forms. It possesses a downward motion that causes decay and disintegration. Tamas brings about ignorance and delusion in the mind and promotes insensitivity, sleep and loss of awareness. It is the principle of materiality or unconsciousness that causes consciousness to become veiled.

Obviously, then, the goal is to make your life as sattvic, as much in the mode of sattva, as possible. It's not easy. We are creatures of habit, and to change habits takes determination and courage. Changing habits means facing resistance from not only yourself, but more challenging still, friends and family members. To make matters worse, it's the nature of the gunas to perpetuate themselves. When you're in a mix of tamas and rajas, you'll appreciate and feel attracted to tamas and rajas. Sattva will seem boring and unattractive. So the initial upgrade from tamas and rajas has to be pushed by your intelligence. It is like breaking a smoking habit. Everyone knows smoking is a deadly habit, but if you're a smoker, your body and mind crave it. To stop smoking, your intelligence has to override the body and mind's call for nicotine. And once you make the leap and your body and mind are no longer addicted to nicotine, you experience a better life and no longer need to force yourself not to smoke. Upgrading your life to sattva-guna takes some effort in the beginning, but you'll experience the benefits of maximizing your material and spiritual potential.

The effects of changing the "mix" of gunas in your life are immediate. It might take you some time to experience the benefits of, say, cultivating wisdom or meditating, but the practical suggestions in this section will give you immediate results.

The Difference Between Actual Spiritual Connection and a Noble Life

There are many ways to make your life better by becoming more sattvic. They make you feel and act so much better that people sometimes confuse spirituality with simply leading a noble, sattvic life.

Being friendly, vegetarian, kind, ecological, compassionate, and just a really good person does not mean you're spiritual. To be truly spiritual, you have to be all these and a lot more. Being spiritual means having a connection with transcendence – more specifically, with God. Remember, *yoga* means "connection" – the connection of the soul with God, or at least with His Brahman energy. Living a life in sattva is the means to maximize your spiritual *potential*, but it's not, in and of itself, spiritual. A noble life is necessary but insufficient for being a true yogi.

On the 3T Path, jnana and bhakti, the last two of the five avenues of perfection, are the truly spiritual components. The first three avenues of perfection are powerful and necessary elements to be able to put jnana and bhakti into practice. Contained in this section are further tips to make you more qualified and apt to practice the five avenues of perfection. Each of these avenues of perfection and each of these tips makes your life better and makes you feel better. And there are benefits from every step you take, no matter the order.

So Full of Yourself, Yet So Empty

One of the greatest obstacles to self-improvement and self-realization is pride. A proud person closes his or her mind to the need to be better, seeking instead confirmation of just how superior he or she is.

Pride—vanity, egocentrism, and even narcissism—can all be deepened by the effects of social media. Every "like" is registered, every follower noted, as one seeks recognition by increasing one's number of views. It's a gigantic competition, and fame can come in a matter of days, even minutes. The natural desire to be seen, heard, and appreciated has expanded to unnatural proportions.

When we're consumed by the desire for confirmation, we risk losing our will to improve. If I'm already so incredible, why should I want to become better? If the only thing lacking is for more people to recognize my greatness, power, beauty, or talent, why should I listen to others—what can I learn from them?

Craving other people's approval generates suffering in the form of anxiety, envy, anger, and insecurity. The fear of being ignored, belittled, forgotten, or excluded hounds attention-seekers.

How can we spot our weaknesses so we can change? The solution is to cultivate modesty. We need modesty to evaluate our faults and channel our natural desire to grow and improve, to seek the advice of others and take in that advice with sincerity and true intent. Before we can take anyone's instructions seriously, we must first have sufficient modesty to understand how much we need and can benefit from them.

Modesty frees you from the burden of dependence on others' approval. This brings peace to the heart. Instead of being anxious for attention and affirmation, you try to honestly evaluate yourself, humbly accepting that you are full of faults and can use all the help you can get.

A gentle but realistic understanding of our failings can guide us to constantly seek to improve. As you compare yourself today to yesterday's version of yourself, you can become more motivated to improve every day.

Drugs and Alcohol

The desire to consume drugs and alcohol is born out of the natural desire to experience a different state of consciousness. They are often ways to relax or break down inhibitions in social settings. If you want to experience a different state of consciousness, it's likely because you're not totally satisfied with your current state of consciousness. Becoming aware that your current state of consciousness is not ideal is good. And unless you're a fully enlightened being, it's correct. What's not so good is taking the cheap and easy way to change it, messing around with the workings of your brain. Returning to the TV example, taking drugs and alcohol won't change the program; it will only change the screen. When the effects wear off, you're back to the same program. In fact, you're now worse off, because you just dulled your brain, got more confused and less focused.

If you really want to be happy, you have to take your consciousness to higher levels, not lower ones. Too often, people take drugs and alcohol to dull an existential ache just as we might take pain killers to dull physical pain. Taking pain killers is a good quick fix, but it's far better to cure the problem causing you pain in the first place. And just as medicine and pain killers often have side effects that bring more suffering, using drugs and alcohol to dull the pain of life brings more suffering and limits your power to seek true transformation.

The path of yoga requires purity and clarity of mind. Further, the goal of Eastern spirituality is to overcome illusion. Drugs and alcohol cloud the mind and deepen our illusion by adding another layer to the already illusory identification of the soul with the body. They will, therefore, have an adverse effect on your path of self-improvement and most certainly on the higher levels of that path leading to self-realization.

Everyone agrees that heavy drinking and binge drinking are bad for your physical health. But you may have heard that moderate drinking is good for you. A closer look at the studies, however, reveals that it's only good for those who have an unhealthy lifestyle and diet in the first place – people who don't exercise and have a diet heavy in fat and animal protein, with little or no fruit or vegetables. For those who have even a slightly healthier lifestyle, with some fruit and vegetables and exercise, alcohol has no positive effect.

Some studies show that it's actually unhealthy to drink any amount of alcohol. Dame Sally Davies, Chief Medical Officer for England, declares, "Drinking any level of alcohol regularly carries a health risk for anyone."[5] The message is strong and clear. The UK government now warns that any level of alcohol consumption increases the risk of several types of cancer. The American Center for Disease Control (CDC) states, "[The 2015-2020 Dietary Guidelines for Americans] do not recommend that individuals who do not drink alcohol start drinking for any reason," putting "do not" in bold. The idea that drinking is okay or even healthy is just advertising by the well-paid spin doctors of the alcohol trade. It's physically, mentally, and spiritually better for you not to drink.

As the National Council on Alcoholism and Drug Dependence states, "Alcohol is a factor in 40% of all violent crimes today, and according to the Department of Justice, 37% of almost 2 million convicted offenders currently in jail, report that they were drinking at the time of their arrest." Further, "80% of offenders abuse drugs or alcohol. Nearly 50% of jail and prison inmates are clinically addicted. Approximately 60% of individuals arrested for most types of crimes test positive for illegal drugs at arrest." In 2014 almost ten thousand people died as victims of drunk driving in the US. Someone might think that they're special and will not commit violence, have someone else act violently toward them, or drive under the influence, but is it worth the risk? And do you want to finance companies who produce these substances that are involved in so much death and suffering? Is this something you want to be a part of?

Caffeine is also a drug. Do yourself a favor and switch over to decaf, or try drinking herbal teas. A Mayo Clinic study showed that people who drank more than four cups of coffee a day had a 21 percent increase in mortality.[6] The risks of caffeine consumption include raised blood pressure, increased risk of heart attacks in young adults, increased risk of incontinence, gout attacks, insomnia, indigestion, headaches and migraines, breast tissue cysts, reduced fertility

---

5 UK Government Chief Medical Officers Guidelines for Alcohol Consumption. 2016.

6 "Caffeine: How much is too much?" www.mayoclinic.org

and increased risk of miscarriage in women, worse menopause symptoms, and greater risk of bone fractures. And caffeine agitates the already agitated mind. The whole purpose of yoga is to pacify the mind, to seek serenity. Caffeine is counterproductive to the goal of achieving a serene and harmonious mind and state of inner peace. As for illegal drugs, the simple fact is that whoever buys them likely becomes a partner and financier of one the most destructive forces in the world today: the drug cartels. Anyone who purchases illegal drugs is helping to kill, terrorize, and enslave millions of people and to corrupt government workers, elected officials, and security personnel all over the world. That is some seriously bad karma.

Vegetarianism

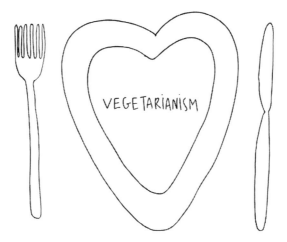

The biggest and most important lifestyle factor for most people interested in advancing on the path of self-improvement and self-realization is not eating meat and eggs.

The Simplest Reason

You'll feel better. Sure, there are exceptions, but almost everyone who becomes vegetarian feels better. If you're not a vegetarian, try it. See if you don't feel better after a month free of meat and eggs. Some say that the feeling is due to just being healthier; others give more precise explanations of the chemicals released when the body is or isn't dealing with meat. Feeling better can also have spiritual and ethical causes. In any case, it's a powerful reason to adopt a vegetarian diet.

Ethics

The number-one dharmic law is ahimsa: not to commit undeserved violence. If you think about it, you'll notice that all acts of immorality, such as theft, lying, and infidelity, have an element of violence. You say that you've been "hurt" by a lie or by the infidelity of a spouse. If someone steals from you, it hurts. By simply being conscious of the pain your actions or words may cause, and carefully avoiding it, you attain a nobler lifestyle, which will come back to you in the form of peace and happiness. This is compassion.

If you're serious about self-improvement, this alone should be sufficient: billions of animals are killed every year. Their lives are full of suffering, and then they are brutally slaughtered. The people who work in this abominable industry themselves suffer horribly, for no matter how dull and cruel someone might be, the effects of causing pain and death all day every day are destructive to human consciousness. This level of brutality in the name of satisfying the tongue is just insane.

We've begun to understand the evils of nationalism, sexism, racism, and religious hatred. The next big ethical challenge for humanity is speciesism: the idea that just because someone is from a different species we have the right to brutalize and abuse them without mercy.

The Environment

The meat industry is destroying the planet:

1. *Greenhouse gases*: According the UN Panel on Climate Change, the meat industry is responsible for more greenhouse gases than the entire transportation sector. All of the world's planes, trucks, trains, cars, motorcycles, and ships combined emit less greenhouse gases than the meat industry.

2. *Water:* By becoming vegetarian, you will save approximately 820 thousand liters of water per year. The production of one kilogram of meat requires about 11,000 liters of water. One kilogram of soy needs only 2,000 liters. Half of the water usage in the US is for feeding animals. Also, the meat industry is polluting underground water reservoirs with the sewage created by the animals, which is mostly left untreated and goes straight into the soil.

3. *Land:* A staggering 30 percent of the planet's surface is being used by the meat industry. The increase in pasture land is the main culprit in the destruction of forests and other natural habitats. In the US, 80 percent of agricultural land is used for the meat industry.

4. *Ocean:* Our oceans are being destroyed, in large part due to over-fishing. And 50 percent of all fishing is done to feed animals destined for slaughter. As unbelievable as it may sound, at the present no other species eats as much fish as do cows.

If you care about the environment, the single most effective measure you can take is to become a vegetarian. Every other measure comes a distant second.

Your Health

There is now sufficient evidence to prove that a plant-based diet is the healthiest option – not just a "feel better" kind of healthy, but a serious "avoid dying of heart disease and cancer" kind of healthy. It's a scientific fact that eating meat and eggs significantly increases your risk of heart disease and a wide range of cancers. Eating a non-vegetarian diet is the equivalent of smoking cigarettes: an unintelligent and dangerous habit.

The good news for non-vegetarians is that the body will heal itself if you stop eating meat, just as lungs can heal even after years of cigarette smoking. Better yet, studies show that a plant-based diet strengthens the body in its fight against cancer and heart disease, and also helps reduce or eliminate diabetes. If you want to learn more of the facts and figures, I recommend the work of Dr. Michael Greger, MD. But here is a brief list for your consideration:

- *Heart Disease:* Vegetarians have 24 percent less risk of heart disease than non-vegetarians.

- *Cancer:* Vegetarians are 40 percent less likely to get cancer than meat-eaters (Thorogood et al, 1994).

- *Lifespan:* A plant-based diet will maximize your longevity. A twelve-year study by Oxford researchers and published in the British Medical Journal showed that vegetarians outlive meat-eaters by six years. Dr. Michael F. Roizen, MD, showed that a vegetarian diet can increase your life by thirteen years.[7]

---

7 *Michael F. Roizen and John La Puma,* The RealAge Diet: Make Yourself Younger with What You Eat *(HarperCollins, 2002).*

- *Weight Control:* The obesity rate in vegans is between 6 and 9 percent, compared to 33.3 percent for non-vegetarians. Non-vegetarians are three to five times as likely to be obese.

- *Toxic Chemicals:* The US Environmental Protection Agency estimates that nearly 95 percent of the pesticide residue in the typical American diet comes from meat, fish, and dairy products. Fish are the worst due to being contaminated by heavy metals, especially mercury, that are not removed by cooking or freezing.

- *Diabetes:* As little as two weeks on a plant-based diet is enough to drastically reduce and even eliminate diabetes. The reduced chance of excess weight on a vegan diet also leads to a reduced risk of diabetes. And people with diabetes are twice as likely to suffer from heart disease and stroke.

- *Blood Pressure:* As reported by the US Heart, Lung and Blood Institute, just increasing the consumption of fruits and vegetables and decreasing the consumption of meat is enough to reduce high blood pressure.

The list goes on. The research is in: it's simply not healthy to eat animals. Ask yourself: Is the supposed taste-bud pleasure of meat-eating worth increasing the risk of cancer or heart disease, having a stroke or getting diabetes, or being overweight and dying younger?

As renowned doctor, author, and clinical researcher Neal Bernard, MD, founder of the Physicians Committee, says, "Meat – any meat – costs lives. It promotes intolerable suffering and disease – not only amongst animals but also for many Americans by raising their risk of heart disease, diabetes, breast cancer, and early death."[8]

Your Body

One explanation for the many health hazards of eating meat is that the human body just wasn't designed for it. We don't have the physiological traits of carnivores or even omnivores; we have a body more like that of herbivores:

- *Teeth and nails:* We have small canines and soft nails. Carnivores and omnivores have large canines and sharp nails.

---

8 *"Meat Consumption and Cancer Risk," Physicians Committee website. www.pcrm.org*

- *Jaws:* Carnivores and omnivores have jaws that move mostly up and down. Humans, like herbivores, have jaws that also move sideways, to grind grains, plants, and nuts.

- *Stomach acids:* Carnivores and omnivores have extremely acidic stomach juices to digest meat and kill dangerous bacteria in meat. In comparison, our stomach's acid is much weaker.

- *Intestine length:* Carnivores and omnivores have short intestinal tracts to avoid meat rotting and causing illness. We have very long intestines, meant for extracting nutrients from plant-based foods and breaking down fibers.

Consciousness

Meat and eggs are foods in tamas. As explained earlier, your body and your mind are connected and your physical choices have a serious and deep impact on your mind and state of consciousness. One of the most important factors in determining the guna influence on your life is your diet. As the saying goes, "You are what you eat." Tamas is the heaviest, darkest material influence. It shuts you down. It makes you brutish. It pushes you toward insensitivity and dullness. These are all the opposite of what you want in order to have a joyous life and maximize your potential. If you're serious about reaching higher and finer levels of consciousness, a meat-free diet is the first step.

Karma

In the previous sections on bhakti and "putting it all together," I explained the importance of making your life a loving offering to God. As part of this great objective, one of the key practices of the 3T Method is offering your food to God before you eat it. This is an exercise in gratitude and a recognition that everything comes from God. By offering our food, we eliminate its karma, just as offering any action to God (karma-yoga) eliminates the karma from the action. The caveat is that God also practices ahimsa, so He does not partake in gratuitous violence or the senseless killing of His innocent children. The foods you can offer to God are those that minimize violence – vegetarian food. Sure, lettuce is killed to be eaten, and so is a carrot. But the level of violence in killing lettuce or a carrot is obviously much less than that of killing an animal. Eating offered vegetarian food, called prasada, means having a zero-karma diet. Even eating vegetarian food that is not offered implicates the eater in negative karma, what to speak of food borne out of violence and death.

Veganism

Veganism involves the further step of not eating dairy. Dairy in itself, however, doesn't negatively affect your consciousness; it's not in tamas. Throughout history, avatars, yogis, and other saintly people have consumed dairy products. No society has been vegan, for the simple reason that there are no reliable sources of B12 in plant foods – only in dairy, meat, and eggs. B12 is an essential vitamin, and its deficiency can cause severe health problems.

Since meat and eggs are in tamas and are outright cruel, the standard diet in the yoga tradition has been lacto-vegetarianism. In traditional Indian culture, dairy cows were lovingly maintained and milked with no violence to them or their calves. Cows were taken care of until their natural death, even after they'd stopped producing milk. In some places, both in India and the West, this is still being done. Milk produced in this way is called "ahimsa milk."

Unfortunately, ahimsa milk is still hard to obtain. The dairy industry overall is cruel, with cows suffering and being killed after a few years – separated from their calves and sold for meat. So there is definitely a strong ethical argument against the use of such dairy products. Dairy can also affect your health negatively, so it's best to restrict dairy consumption, even if you have access to ahimsa products.

These days, with the advent of B12 vitamin supplements and fortified vegan foods, there are no exclusive health benefits in consuming dairy products. And with the scarcity of "ahimsa milk," veganism is the preferred option for those seeking to maximize their physical and spiritual well-being.

Cultural Consumption

Every song you hear, text you read, image you see, film you watch, performance you attend – what I call your cultural consumption –affects you, for better or for worse. You somehow have to process that influence. It may affect your behavior. For example, heavy metal music might make you feel angry or physically agitated. Romantic songs and movies may cause you to feel that you need to find an idyllic romantic partner. Documentaries might make you think harder about something. If you listen to baroque music, you might feel calmer. If you listen to mantra chants, you may feel more spiritual or relaxed. And if you hear devotional music, you are more likely to feel peaceful and remember God. It all affects you and shapes who you are and how you think.

Knowing this, you should be careful about your cultural consumption. It should become a means to make your life better, a tool to chisel out an improved version of yourself, not an anchor to the version of you that you're trying to transform. You have to be aware of what aspects of your nature your cultural consumption is stimulating. Is it stimulating your desire for the fantasy paradigm, or to be more selfish, violent, or greedy? Or is it helping you become a better person?

In yoga terms, what is the prevalent guna of your cultural diet? Just as cultural consumption in sattva makes you feel better, healthier, more peaceful, and fully able to grow spiritually, cultural consumption in rajas, and especially in tamas, will have a negative impact on your overall well-being.

Sure, we should have fun; it's part of our natural dharma. But the kind of entertainment you choose will have an impact on you. It's like eating. Once in a while, you may want to eat some kind of junk food. But your body will have to process it long after the fun is over. It's the same with what you consume with your eyes and ears. The more sattvic your cultural consumption, the better off you'll be.

Cleanliness and Order

Two of the major qualities of sattva are cleanliness and order. I'm sure you've felt the impact of cleanliness and order on your mind. When you take a shower after waking up or coming home from work, you feel lighter. When you clean and organize your living space, you feel better. When you put on fresh clothes or even just change your bedsheets, you can feel a positive impact. And the opposite is also true. You may have entered a particularly dirty and messy household and felt a negative, somewhat depressing sensation. You may have entered a run-down or dirty bar or nightclub and experienced heaviness and dullness.

Cleanliness is often recommended in sacred yoga literature. It is mentioned in the *Yoga Sutras* as the first order of business for those desiring to advance in yoga. In the *Bhagavad-gita* it is listed by Krishna as one of the "divine" qualities necessary for upliftment. In the Christian tradition we find the famous instruction "Cleanliness is next to godliness."

A relevant practical consequence of this can be felt in the all-important practice of meditation. You'll meditate better with a clean body, in a clean and uncluttered environment (or in nature), and in clean clothes.

When you sleep, you sweat and drool. Ancient Indian medicine, Ayurveda, teaches that during sleep your body gets rid of toxins through the skin. Thus, a daily morning shower is key to cleanliness in your life. Another shower after a long day out is also helpful. Taking your shoes off at the door is also important. Dr. Charles Gerba from the University of Arizona identified 440 thousand units of dangerous germs in a shoe worn for only two weeks. A public toilet floor contains two million bacteria per square inch. This is not something you want to bring into your home. Beware also of sharing touchscreens, as they harbor a staggering amount of germs. The kitchen, especially, should be a place of strict cleanliness, though it has been found to contain more germs than any other place in the house.

Regarding order, researchers at the Princeton University Neuroscience Institute have shown that clutter lessens your ability to focus and process information – to organize your thoughts. A UCLA study showed that clutter overloads your senses and makes you feel stressed. Clutter can also be present in our lives in digital format – emails, messages, and computer files, which can affect our consciousness.

Simplicity

The benefits of simplicity and removing clutter can be taken a step further when you remove existential clutter from your life. The basic idea is that the less you have, the less you have to worry about and the more peaceful you will be. And as Krishna says in the *Bhagavad-gita*, "How can there be happiness without peace?"

You are limited in every way. You only have so much energy, so much mental power, so much money . . . and there are only twenty-four hours in a day. So you have to carefully decide how to use those limited resources. A simple-living movement is growing throughout the world, as people finally understand that less is more. When you minimize the amount of stuff you have, you experience increasing freedom and well-being.

The first rule is to buy only what you need. This becomes easier when you are equipped with the knowledge of dharma. Your financial resources should be used as a means to execute your dharma. Knowing what to buy becomes clear when you think like this. It's like working for a business or holding a government position and being accountable for every penny you spend. You can have this kind of seriousness in your own life, where the "business" is executing your dharma. Hold yourself accountable and always ask if you really need something before you buy it. "Is this going to further the execution of my dharma?" "Is buying this part of my dharma?" You are accountable. The money isn't really yours. It was entrusted to you, and how you spend it will affect your mind, your well-being, and your future.

Buying on impulse, influenced by a pretty window display or fancy ad campaign, is a sign of mental weakness. It's a waste of not only your resources, but also the planet's.

Invest in experiences, not things. Studies show that this will make you happier. An experience becomes an integral part of who you are, whereas an object, no matter how much you like it, is always external to you. And you can share similar experiences with others more deeply than similar products.

Switch off and seek solitude to cultivate simplicity. Mainstream society is driven by consumerism. Ads are everywhere, bombarding you with suggestions to buy things that you don't actually need. To create a simple-living mentality, give yourself some space from that disturbing influence.

Taking Care of Your Body

Mens sana in corpore sano – a healthy body will help you have a healthy mind. The body is a complex machine and needs proper maintenance. Exercise makes you feel better. You can sweat away the tamas (lethargy, dullness, heaviness). Exercise has many benefits:

- Helps control your weight

- Reduces the risk of heart disease

- Can lower blood pressure

- Improves your cholesterol levels

- Reduces the risk of cancers

- Strengthens your bones and muscles

- Helps you maintain your balance

- Improves your mood.

"Exercising at very light levels reduced deaths from any cause by 14 percent", Dr. Chi Pang Wen discovered. The same study showed that a mere fifteen minutes of exercise a day increases life expectancy by three years.[9]

If you think you're short on time for this essential natural dharma, look into high-intensity interval training workouts (HIITs). As little as ten minutes of exercise can have a significant benefit. I also recommend calisthenics and bodyweight-and-suspension training, which uses only movements, ropes, bars, and the weight of your body. These exercises are more natural and provide a more comprehensive workout than those using weights and machines.

Hatha yoga or any yoga of asanas is an excellent overall workout, but it will keep you fit only if you practice a wide range of asanas several times per week, preferably daily. Otherwise, it's best to complement your practice with other forms of exercise. Tai Chi is a beautiful form of exercise that outside of China doesn't get the traction or attention it deserves.

---

9 *"Minimum amount of physical activity for reduced mortality and extended life expectancy: a prospective cohort study." The University of Texas MD Anderson Cancer Center Department of Epidemiology (Chi Pang Wen et al)*

And there is walking. Walking is an underrated form of exercise that has tremendous health benefits and a very low risk of injury. Try doing mantra meditation (taught at the end of the book in the 3T Method) while walking. It's called a "japa walk" and is an excellent body and spirit workout.

These are only a few suggestions. There is a huge range of exercise options for how to stay fit and healthy. Choose whatever works for you!

Taking Sleep Seriously

Sleep may seem like a luxury or, to some, a waste of time. But it's essential for your well-being. As previously mentioned, sleep is part of your natural dharma. Krishna says in the *Bhagavad-gita* that a yogi should not sleep too much or too little. These days, the danger for most people is in sleeping too little. There are just too many distractions, too much work, and too much mental agitation. Over one third of Americans suffer from sleep deprivation. Here are some dangers caused by insufficient sleep:

1. *Accidents:* There are thousands of deaths each year caused by road accidents. Other kinds of accidents as well, including the 1979 nuclear accident at Three Mile Island, the massive 1989 Exxon Valdez oil spill in Alaska, and the 1986 nuclear meltdown at Chernobyl, have sleep deprivation as a factor.

2. *Reduced brain power:* Lack of sleep leads to less concentration, attention, alertness, and problem-solving ability. Studies show that being seriously sleep deprived makes you just as impaired as being legally drunk. Lack of sleep also affects your memory and makes your more depressed.

3. *Poor overall health:* Insufficient sleep can be a factor in heart problems, high blood pressure, stroke risk, and diabetes.

4. *Unhealthy appearance:* Lack of sleep ages your skin due to the release of excess cortisol, which breaks down collagen, the protein that keeps skin smooth.

5. *Impaired judgment:* Lack of sleep affects your ability to judge things correctly, including the effects of that lack of sleep. Sleep-deprived people do poorly on mental-alertness and performance tests but think they're doing fine.

Tips for getting good sleep include:

1. Be in bed by ten p.m.

2. Keep the room quiet, cool, and very dark.

3. Accept sleep as your natural dharma. You need and deserve it. When it's time to sleep, focus on just relaxing; don't let your mind go over problems or get caught up in planning.

4. Just before you go to sleep, or if you wake up at night, keep lights dim. Bright lights make your brain think it's time to wake up. Bright screens from your phone, tablet, or TV will also wake you up. Your brain releases melatonin when it's dark, helping you sleep better.

Breathing exercises, *pranayama* in Sanskrit, also help. Dr. Andrew Weil made international news in 2015 when he claimed that the 4-7-8 breathing technique could get you to sleep in one minute.[10] The technique is simple:

1. Exhale completely through your mouth, making a whoosh sound.

2. Close your mouth and inhale quietly through your nose to a mental count of four.

3. Hold your breath for a count of seven.

4. Exhale completely through your mouth, making a whoosh sound to a count of eight.

5. This is one breath. Now inhale again and repeat the cycle three more times for a total of four breaths.

Power napping can also be beneficial, especially if you don't get enough sleep at night. A ten-to-twenty-minute nap in the middle of the day can recover energy, give you superior memory recall, and increase alertness.

Dangers of the Tongue

The most treacherous sense organ is the tongue. There are two reasons for this: 1) the tongue drives you to eat and consume all sorts of things that are

---

10 *"Breathing Exercises: 4-7-8 Breath," www.drweil.com.*

detrimental to your mental and spiritual well-being and can even kill you prematurely and 2) the tongue allows you to talk a lot of nonsense and say hateful things.

We've gone through the dangers of eating non-vegetarian food and the disadvantages of consuming alcohol, coffee, and other drugs. But what about the dangers of useless chatter?

Talking consumes your attention and mental energy. You can do a lot of others things, like driving, running, watching a movie, or working out with your mind somewhere else, on any subject you choose. Talking, though, really demands your attention. Anything else you try to do at the same time will take second place. Because it's so intense, what you say will have a strong impact on your own consciousness. It will also affect those who listen to you, but only to the degree that they're paying attention. As the speaker, you're the most affected, because so much of your attention is going to the act of speaking.

If you talk nonsense, you'll be contaminated by that nonsense. You are creating your own negative cultural consumption. Worse, if you speak hateful things, you pollute your mind with negative energy, which eventually comes back to worsen your life to some degree. It's all garbage that you'll have to process and that will affect who you are and what you experience in life.

The urge to talk is very strong. Just observe any situation with more than one person. People can't stop blabbing away – often with hours of useless chit-chat and gossip. It's a real challenge, and of great importance, to control this urge.

You can stop this blabbing by slowly trying to control your tongue. First try to notice when you're talking unnecessarily. Then try to curtail your urge. Shorten or cut off your speech. Maybe you need to adjust your workplace or avoid social settings where this kind of practice is common. Also, don't let yourself be a victim of someone's ceaseless chatter or complaining. Kindly but firmly excuse yourself. If you can, be open about it and say that you're trying to improve yourself and overcome your own habit of talking too much. If possible, make a private, personal vow to avoid engaging in gossip and saying hateful things.

Hurtful speech is a disaster. You can ruin relationships and cause enduring pain to others, usually those closest to you. One way or another, this pain will come back to you. You'll feel embarrassed and sad for having spoken like this, but as much as you may apologize, the damage will have been done. Your words will be remembered by those you hurt – and probably by you.

These days, we also have to extend the warning of the dangers of the tongue to our thumbs. Much gossip and useless, even hateful speech happens in the form of texting or typing. The same principles apply.

Krishna describes the perfection of speech in the *Bhagavad-gita*. It's a lofty goal, but one that you can strive to achieve. He says that the gold standard of speech meets four criteria: 1) it's true, 2) it's pleasing, 3) it's beneficial, and 4) it's not disturbing. If what you're about to say doesn't meet these criteria, try silence.

Silence

Silence really is golden. Plato's axiom is perfect: "Wise men speak because they have something to say, fools because they have to say something." There is far too much going into people's ears – too much talk, music, TV, podcasts, radio, videos, and traffic noises – a major reason why people are so confused, agitated, and disharmonious.

Silence helps pacify and focus your mind and is thus a great ally in achieving inner peace. In contemplative silence you can discover yourself and uncover and heal old emotional traumas and, if you've qualified yourself for it with jnana and bhakti, enter into divine communion. Silence will at the very least let you organize your thoughts, help your creativity, and give you clarity of mind. UCLA researchers have found that silence aids your brain's development and your ability to process information.

Contemplative silence is a powerful tool for those seeking self-improvement and self-realization. You should experience it every day, at different times during the day, even for as little as one minute at a time.

Sex as a Sacred Act

Sex is a serious matter. It's the ultimate act of intimacy. Sex creates an exchange of subtle energy, which can affect your consciousness very deeply. Because it's such a powerful practice, it can cause profound positive or negative effects. It can take you to greater inner peace and harmony, or it can cause enormous suffering.

When it's practiced within a sacred union, sex is a sacred act. In such a context, it can be practiced as a confirmation of that union – of sharing, mutual care, and the deep exclusive intimacy of a couple, who are sworn to each other. Outside of this sacred union, sex can be the cause of serious physical, emotional, and social problems.

Promiscuity is dangerous, putting you at a greater risk of contracting sexually transmitted diseases, including HPV, HIV, chlamydia, and cancers of the mouth, cervix, and anus. It also takes an emotional toll. Promiscuity has been linked to depression, an inability to have healthy relationships, and risky behavior.

The simple fact is that sex between a male and female can lead to procreation. Even with all the anti-conception technology available, unwanted pregnancies abound, including among the well-educated and prosperous. According to the Center for Disease Control and Prevention, 50 percent of all pregnancies in the US in 2006 were unintended. Among teenagers the rate was a staggering 80 percent.[11]

The consequences of an unwanted pregnancy are serious. A new human life has been started at the moment of conception. Abortion is a heinous and immoral act, the killing of one's own child. And when sex happens outside of a loving relationship, it's unlikely the mother and father will stay together in harmony or serve the child together. More likely, the mother will have to bear the brunt of single-parenthood, and all too often the father, shamelessly, does little or nothing.

This is dangerous and destructive for both the child and society: "[T]he most reliable indicator of violent crime in a community is the proportion of fatherless families... Children from single-parent families are more prone than children from two-parent families to use drugs, be gang members, be expelled from school, be committed to reform institutions, and become juvenile murderers" (NCJRS, US Department of Justice, Sadler, 1997).

Raising a child is an intense responsibility and it's extremely challenging for one parent to do it alone. It's far better when there are two parents or better yet, as the African proverb says, a whole village. Sex between a fertile male and female should always be regarded as an act of possible procreation and, as such, practiced only by those willing to accept the consequence as a couple, with love and responsibility.

Restricting sex to a sacred union safeguards your well-being. It protects you from disease, the risk of having a child with someone you might not even like, and in the case of adultery, often a broken family. The perfection of sex is the conscious and sober act of a couple invoking a child. This is its most beautiful and divine form. Sex within a sacred union protects you from the frustration and emotional numbing that arises from having undue intimacy with a person with whom you are not truly bonding. Making sex an exclusive act of intimacy with the person you've chosen to share your life with makes it an important expression of your love and commitment.

Vision of Oneness and Service

In spiritual terms, we are all one. Not one in the sense of a single entity, but one in the sense of all being transcendental souls. On the spiritual platform there is no such thing as a rich or poor soul, a smart or dumb soul, or a beautiful or ugly soul. All souls are divine sparks, perfect in who they are. We are all equally pure and perfect and equally loved by our Mother and Father, Radha-Krishna.

In the material world no two people are equally qualified; no two are the same.

---

11 *"Unintended Pregnancy Prevention," CDC website, www.cdc.gov.*

But these differences are temporary and superficial. Ultimately, every soul will regain its pure transcendental state.

The spiritualist can see every living being in oneness. "With equal vision everywhere, the yoga-linked self sees Self in all creatures and all creatures in Self," Krishna explains in the *Bhagavad-gita*.[12] A yogi will recognize that no matter what apparent external differences there are, every living creature is deeply bonded to them.

This is especially important because hatred is based on perceiving differences. Differences in nationality, race, sex, religion, social class are all illusory, insignificant considerations that lead those with troubled minds to commit violence. Not only humans, but every living creature, is part of the same family. It is thus in everyone's best interest to work in cooperation, valuing our oneness over our superficial differences.

As souls, our only business is to love and thus to serve. In the state of mind of identifying with every other living creature, the natural tendency is to develop the mood of service, which in Sanskrit is called *seva*. Service, again, is the natural outcome of love. When you're feeling selfish and mundane, you want to be served. When you expand your consciousness and become spiritual, you want to serve. It's that simple. This service will happen according to your dharma. It may bring great fame or not even be recognized. It may bring wealth or cause you to lose all your wealth. It may be easy or very troublesome. But none of these considerations matter, for they are all external and have nothing to do with the real you. What really matters to the soul is that which pertains to the soul: the experience of being occupied in your dharma, in the mood of loving service in divine communion. Though bliss is not the objective of love and service, it is the consequence.

The Company You Keep

The gunas' greatest influence on you comes through the company you keep. You are deeply influenced by those you keep close. This can become a problem if you're seeking transformation. The people closest to you might not like seeing you change, and if this is the case, you won't change if you don't make some adjustments to your company and the habits and mindset they represent.

As George Washington said, "Better alone than in bad company." Solitude is powerful in that it frees you from the influence of other people. You get to be yourself, by yourself, with yourself. It's important to create these moments in life to get to know yourself better. We cannot live in complete

---

12 H.D Goswami, *A Comprehensive Guide to Bhagavad-gita with Literal Translation,* Chapter 6, Verse 29. (Torchlight Publishing, 2015).

isolation, but such moments can serve to strengthen your resolve to seek better company.

Almost every serious spiritualist has to come to terms with this problem of adjusting one's social circle to his or her new reality. It takes patience and courage, but it really is essential. You start by turning down some invitations to situations no longer attractive to you, such as places where people go to get drunk, hook up, or just talk nonsense, and you gradually seek out a new crowd more aligned with your newfound principles of transformation and spirituality. Gradually, you have to find your new "vibe tribe."

It can be helpful to seek out gatherings or events with those who share your spiritual goals and practices, to get association with like-minded serious practitioners. There are festivals, kirtans (mantra shows or group chants), classes, and temples you can visit. Be careful, though, to avoid fanaticism or cultish behavior. There is always a potential for abuse in spiritual organizations, so keep your intelligence and preserve your independence.

Respect, serve, and be nice to everyone, but choose carefully with whom you want to keep close association. That person's mentality will affect your mentality, and vice-versa; you will share your states of mind. The quickest way to attain transformation is to seek the company of those who have the qualities you wish to assimilate.

A Culture of Respect

One of the biggest obstacles to growth is pride. Pride blocks your ability to see your faults and learn from others. It fuels self-centeredness, competition, conceit, and arrogance and inhibits your devotion. One way to deal with pride is to practice respect. When you show respect, you are showing appreciation. You're expressing the view that a person has value and deserves your appreciation.

Because pride is so damaging to any path of self-improvement and self-realization, developing humility and abandoning self-centeredness is crucial. This is certainly the case on the path of yoga. As part of the practice of humility, those on this path cultivate respect and demonstrate it through different hand and body gestures.

The famous "namaste" greeting, with a slight bowing of the body and palms pressed together, is a form of showing your respect. Its literal translation is, "I bow to you" (not "the God in me bows down to the God in you"). Bhakti yogis like to use the holy names in their greetings and so will often say "Hare Krishna" instead of "namaste".

More formal is offering respect by touching your forehead to the floor, on your hands and knees, for when you meet a spiritual teacher or advanced practitioner in an appropriate setting. The most formal show of respect in the yoga tradition is called the dandavat, meaning "stick-like" – when you lie fully prostrate, with eight parts of your body (two toes, two knees, two palms, chest, and forehead) touching the floor. This is appropriate when you see your spiritual teacher, or a Deity in a temple. Using your whole body to offer respect to God and great souls is a great way to invoke mercy and growth. It's a powerful asana for overcoming pride and developing humility.

A culture of respect makes social dealings more fluid. It generates a peaceful atmosphere and helps avoid crass and inappropriate behavior. It helps you become humbler, more grateful, and more inclined to serve. It makes it easier to appreciate others.

Accepting a Spiritual Teacher

There are a variety of spiritual objectives and numerous techniques for achieving them. Unless you choose one path and stick to it until you find a better one, you won't advance much. Cherry-picking techniques and teachings but never committing yourself to one path is ineffective. I've been a spiritualist and have observed spiritualists for twenty-five years, and it's an inescapable fact that you have to commit to one path. Later, if you need to, you can adopt another; you should always keep an open mind and use your intelligence. But if you don't have a specific goal and a daily set of practices, transmitted and embodied by a bona fide spiritual teacher, you'll coast along, trying to please your own mind. You'll get lazy. One person says you should meditate twenty minutes a day minimum, using mantras. Another says that five intervals of silence for one minute per day are enough. Yet another says that you should practice mindfulness but ignore God. And so on. If you don't commit to one path, your mind will tell you do one thing one day, another thing the next, and most days nothing at all. There will not be any clarity of vision or purpose. And without a fixed daily practice, called sadhana, progress is very slow. In order to advance steadily in your process of transformation and self-realization, it's essential to choose one path and one main spiritual teacher.

Westerners are relatively new to the whole concept of accepting a spiritual teacher, or guru, and there is sometimes culture shock, an awkward merging of cultures. Guru is Sanskrit for "teacher." It doesn't mean "spiritual teacher"; a grammar or martial arts teacher is also a guru. Since spirituality is the most important teaching, it's understandable that you would offer the spiritual teacher the highest respect. Still, we should not forget that the guru is a teacher. He or she is human and more than likely still learning and evolving, even if some claim to be perfectly enlightened.

In the West, many people's first impressions of Indian gurus have been of high-profile charismatic figures, not all of them genuine. Some of them really put on a show, and later their ulterior motives of seeking fame, sex, and/or wealth became apparent. Several came in the '60s and '70s, when the hippie culture was in full swing and people were inclined to the exotic. This sometimes led to a garish or cultish mood in which the guru was seen as more than a teacher; he was a savior, beyond the human condition, or God come in human form, free of all mistakes. This irrational approach created unhealthy personality cults.

Too much or too little of any good thing is bad. There are several problems with taking the natural desire to honor and appreciate the spiritual teacher too far:

1. *Regression into childishness:* Some people give up their responsibility and project onto a charismatic spiritual teacher the role of a mother or father, to the point where they become like children, incapable of making decisions without consulting the spiritual teacher. They think that this person can counsel them on marriage, finances, work, and politics. What's worse, many spiritual teachers gladly accept or even encourage this power over their students. This creates an unhealthy and dangerous relationship. Sexual and psychological abuse and profiteering all start with this approach.

2. *Unreal expectations:* People may expect the spiritual master to either drag them to enlightenment or just bless them into perfection. But it doesn't work like that. The grace of the spiritual master is knowledge. He or she can bestow knowledge and show the example. It requires a serious and qualified student to put the instructions into practice and gradually, over the course of his or her life, overcome his or her faults, illusions, and attachments. There are no shortcuts. Beware of the charlatan who offers shortcuts to eternal spiritual perfection, especially for a price.

3. *Star-struck mentality:* A student should not cultivate a fan mentality or become giddy over a teacher's charisma and fame. Before committing him- or herself, he or she should soberly analyze the spiritual teacher's moral qualities, teachings, qualifications, and knowledge of his or her spiritual lineage. There are plenty of people with enormous charisma and fame who are spiritually bankrupt. These traits do not prove a teacher's quality.

As Westerners, we tend to tone things down. What's the most respect you've had for a teacher or mentor? Take that up a notch and apply it to your spiritual teacher. You don't have to have giant pictures of your teacher in your home or wear t-shirts with an image of his or her face. If you have an altar, the main focus should be on God, not on your spiritual teacher. A genuine teacher will be pleased to see this. He or she will not have any need for you to fawn at his or her feet. The overall mood should be of appreciation and friendly respect with a willingness to serve – not unthinking, tear-streaming awe and adulation. Getting down to earth about your spirituality and your spiritual teacher is healthy. It's also practical and rational. There is no need to get so mystical and weird about it.

Choose a spiritual teacher and dedicate yourself to his or her teachings. Respect him or her and understand your enormous debt of gratitude. Understand that the best way to serve your spiritual teacher is to advance strongly on the path he or she is teaching, so you too can one day become a spiritual teacher and pay your debt forward.

True Success and Prosperity

The world desperately needs a new standard for success and prosperity. The idea that success means money and fame and that prosperity means having lots of things – much more than we can possibly need – is just insane. It misses two obvious truths: 1) that the true standard for success is happiness and well-being, and 2) that happiness has little to do with money, fame, or owning things.

This message is so obvious and simple that it is expressed over and over in popular stories for both children and adults – happiness comes from doing the right thing and in love and service, not from having power, money, or possessions. It's one of those things that everyone knows but few follow. People torture themselves in stressful, grueling work for decades, chasing a toxic pot of gold. We are destroying the planet and ruining our lives in a misguided search for happiness in consumerism and social status.

Buying things and accumulating possessions will not make you happy. "Despite the claims of consumer culture to the contrary," states Tim Kasser, professor of psychology at Knox University and author of two books on materialism and consumerist culture, "what research has shown in literally dozens of studies is that the more that people prioritize materialistic values, the less happy they are, the less satisfied they are with their lives, the less vital and energetic they feel, the less likely they are to experience pleasant emotions like happiness and contentment and joy, the more depressed they are, the more anxious they are, the more they experience unpleasant emotions like fear and anger and sadness, [and] the more likely they are to engage in the use of substances like cigarettes and alcohol."[13]

True success and prosperity are achieved inside, not outside. The good news is that it's totally up to you. It has nothing to do with luck, where you were born, your IQ, your beauty or strength, the government, or the economy – it's just you, as you are, right now. All perfection and true prosperity are yours to be had by following the path of self-improvement and self-realization.

---

13 *"Materially False: Q&A with Time Kasser about the Pursuit of the Good through Goods,"* The Psych Report, *September 9, 2014, www.thepsychreport.com/conversations/ materially-false-qa-tim-kasser-pursuit-good-goods/*

PART 4
DEALING WITH
LIFE'S PROBLEMS

PART 4 – DEALING WITH LIFE'S PROBLEMS

The 3T Path gives you all the tools and knowledge you need to diminish and even overcome life's problems. This power comes from the fact that you'll be dealing with life's ups and downs from the inside out. You have very little power to change the outside facts of life, but you can develop total and complete power to change the inside – how you deal with life. Taking control of your life from the inside out is the focus and secret of the entire path of yoga and the key to overcoming or at least lessening your suffering.

What Problem?

Actually there are no problems. Think about it: what you call a problem is when something happened that you didn't expect or desire. Where was this expectation and desire? In the future. Was it realistic? Apparently not. It was a fantasy. This is at the core of the 3T Path: changing from the fantasy paradigm to the life paradigm. Live life as it is, here and now.

And what you have here and now are challenges: from the smallest, like getting out of bed, taking a shower, and meditating for a while; to larger ones, like dealing with a difficult client or fighting off a bad cold; to epic ones, like dealing with a great loss or the death of a loved one. But that's life: a series of challenges, right from the beginning. You had the challenge of dealing with birth, of learning to crawl, of needing sleep and motherly comfort. And it never stopped: first day of school, sharing your toys, sports, school, puberty, social lifenon-stop challenges. This is just the way life is.

What you call a problem is just another challenge – life happening, as it always happens. There are no problems, just reality. And if it is different from what you expected or wanted, you can see how wrong you were in having expectations and undue attachments, living in the future instead of the present. What you call a problem has at the very least the benefit of bringing you back to the here and now and making you focus on your action and being yourself, exercising your wisdom and devotion.

Accept, Be Thankful, Trust, and Make It an Offering

You can prepare yourself to deal with any challenge with a four-step process: 1) accept, 2) be thankful, 3) trust, and 4) make it an offering.

First comes the hardest step: accepting the challenge. Embrace it. You won't make any progress until you do.

The worst thing you can do is lament. Only victims lament. Don't pity yourself; don't complain. Don't grumble about how unjust the world is, how you think God has abandoned you, or how evil someone is. Don't waste your precious time with this. Nothing good will come of it. Even if you are dealing with the most epic challenge, it still doesn't help for you to lament and wallow in sadness and depression.

Once you've overcome lamentation and have accepted the challenge, next comes gratitude. Remember, gratitude is a powerful tool; use it to deal with life's challenges. Be thankful. This may seem strange at first, but it's both effective and empowering. Be thankful that you have a chance to learn and grow. Be thankful something worse didn't happen. Be thankful for being alive and in good consciousness to deal with whatever challenges you face. Most of all, be thankful for the challenge itself. If you study people's lives, you'll see that it's the biggest, most epic challenges that lead people to greatness and success. Facing these challenges, you enter a zone of self-discovery and self-mastery that would otherwise be unattainable.

In a state of acceptance and gratitude, you can now lay your trust in God. If you haven't yet worked on your devotion, you can trust in the universe or "providence." Trust that what's happening to you is exactly what you need, what is ultimately best for everyone involved. And trust reality; it means you well. There is purpose in everything, and nothing happens by chance. There is a force of pure goodness controlling your destiny. Trust that this force is in action as it lays down the challenges for you to face.

Lastly, make your response an offering. Don't desire some future outcome. Don't create undue attachments. Let it go. Do your best, here and now, from this point on. You're not in it for the results. The primary focus is the act itself. Just do your best with what life has given you, one step at a time.

Now you're ready to deal with anything that comes your way.

Dharma Is Your Guide

Whatever comes your way, the solution is based on your dharma. Unexpected challenges are dharma shifts. You have to reconfigure your actions according to your new set of dharmas.

For example, getting fired from a job is a huge dharma shift. Your occupational dharma just got put on hold. Instead you have a new dharma: how to fill the gap. For that, you analyze your other dharmas. Are you single? Do you need to make money? Are you old enough to retire? Were you in the wrong vocation? Maybe this is your chance to go back to college or learn a new trade that expresses your true nature. Maybe it's your chance to give yourself some time off and travel. What might have seemed like a problem can in time become a natural and desirable adjustment.

It's not about what is easiest or most fun or will impress others. It's about who you are and how you can use each challenge to be the best person you can be, the truest to yourself.

The first time I used this technique, I had to give a talk in Brasilia, about 250 km from our yoga resort, Pandavas Paradise, in Alto Paraíso, Chapada dos Veadeiros. I had just finished speaking when I got a call from our groundskeeper. He told me that there had been a big grassland fire and we had lost an entire building in the complex. It was a sizeable loss. Rather than plunge into lamentation and despair, however, I reflected on my years of practice and study in yoga and was able to ask myself, "Okay, what now? What is my duty?" In this case, it was to rebuild. I just got into that. That was a new aspect of my dharma of running the resort: rebuilding the guesthouse as soon as possible. "God giveth, and God taketh away," I told myself. "Don't worry about it." The material loss, the challenge in gathering funds, and the details of the new construction all became part of my occupational dharma, not a source of sadness or despair.

So, first look at your dharma. Take your new situation, the challenge, and consider what is expected of you. See how it changes your duties, how it affects how you live, and thus what new actions are required. Lamenting or worrying about what might ensue does not help. Get your mind in the here and now and identify your duty. Sometimes you have only to pray and be detached and there is no action required on your part. Other times a challenge may bring a whole new set of duties, like when you learn that you're going to be a parent or that you'll have to deal with a long-term illness. Using mindfulness to focus on your dharma will ground you, guide you step-by-step, free your mind from despair and anxiety, and reestablish your inner peace.

It's Never Too Much

You'll never get more than you can handle, but you'll need all your potential to deal with epic challenges, and that includes your spiritual strength. Some challenges are so difficult that you will not be able to overcome them without spiritual wisdom and a mature relationship with God.

As you advance spiritually, you'll also develop detachment. You'll be less bothered by adversity or thrilled by good outcomes. You'll understand that you're not your body and that all living beings are eternal souls, immune to any material situation and safely under the watch of our loving Father. You'll understand that nothing belongs to you, that whatever you have is only on loan. Ultimately, you'll understand that as a soul, you require nothing from this world, as you lack nothing. You are complete and whole as you are – an eternal and unchangeable fact of existence. You have zero to lose, zero to fear.

When the going gets rough, remember who you truly are and what's really going on. This takes spiritual practice and advancement, but it's available to you if you work for it and to the same degree that you advance, it will reduce the impact and suffering of all the challenges you face.

Adversity Is Unavoidable; Suffering Is Optional

Adversity is unavoidable; it's part of life. It doesn't matter who you are or what you have. Everyone has to deal with adversities, both large and small. But the great news is that suffering is optional.

You might think that suffering is something forced on you from the outside or that it is the natural result of a miserable event. If you stop and think about it, however, you'll see that suffering is entirely self-imposed.

You and you alone create your own suffering as your mind refuses to synchronize with reality. All suffering is a result of your mind not being aligned with reality. The greater the difference, the more you suffer. The more you grab onto your fantasy, the more suffering you'll experience in living a reality that doesn't correspond.

The path to diminishing or even overcoming your suffering lies in following the steps of acceptance, gratitude, trust, and engagement in enlightened action, mindfully and according to your dharma. This brings your mind away from fantasy and to reality. It puts you in harmony with what's really going on in your life.

Every situation, no matter how terrible, is a chance to deepen your spiritual consciousness and develop grit.

Some adverse situations come with hidden advantages. How many times have you experienced that not having your wish fulfilled turned out to be the best thing that could have happened? Has something seemingly bad, like being rejected by someone or being fired, ended up opening new doors in your life? As the saying goes, "Everything God does is good."

You can change the world to a very limited degree, but you can drastically change your mind and how it interprets reality. Even as you try to adjust your material circumstances according to your dharmic duties, you must stay in harmony with the situation as it is, in the here and now, making the best of whatever situation you find yourself in.

Suicide

Sometimes adversity is so great, a challenge is so epic, that suicide seems like an attractive – or the only – option. This, of course, is a terrible mistake. Human life is so precious and rare, such a great blessing. It is an opportunity to discover who you truly are and to free yourself from suffering forever.

Two noble qualities of those considering suicide are their detachment and their courage to change. Still, someone considering suicide should use this power to kill not one's body, but one's bad habits, attachments, and painful mental processes.

Neither the body nor the world is the problem. The problem is always within. Since we carry our subtle body, which includes our mind, to the next incarnation, suicide will be of no use. Our troubled mind will accompany us to the next life. By using the techniques and tools of the 3T Path, anyone can experience massive transformation. No one has to suffer uselessly or without end.

How to Deal with the Death of a Loved One

One of life's most difficult challenges is the death of a loved one. We are, as souls, loving creatures. Love means service. Service requires action and personal interaction. So when you are no longer able to interact lovingly with someone, you feel a loss. And to achieve closure, you must recognize and honor that loss.

You can offset your suffering in this situation by looking at things from another angle. To love purely means to see things from the point of view of the beloved. From the point of view of the departed loved one, death is not a problem. That soul has moved on, by the grace of God, to another, better situation – better, at the least, in the sense of being better suited to the advancement of that soul. The soul feels no pain of separation; it has moved on. Neither do you feel any pain of separation from the people you loved and who loved you in your previous lives. So the departed is doing just fine. That soul is eternally alive and well, starting out a new adventure in a new body.

In a sense, you should be happy to know that your loved one is off on a new cycle of life, not feeling any pain from having left you and not suffering the loss of his or her previous life.

And if that person attained enlightenment in love of God, then his or her death was a glorious moment – a graduation ceremony like no other. Freedom from the jail of samsara. The achievement of eternal bliss in loving play with God in His transcendental abode.

We are all going to die. It is the only thing certain in life. You should not live in illusion, fearing death, yours or your loved ones'. Rather, you should cherish each day, each moment, knowing that it may be your last. If you do your best at every moment to love those around you, with awareness of the impermanence of everything material and the eternality of everything spiritual, the challenge of dealing with the loss of a loved one will be greatly diminished.

Forgiveness

The inevitable adversities of life often come in the form of someone else's action. From accidently stepping on your toes to outright brutal physical aggression, people will do things to you, directly or indirectly, that you do not like.

The low-consciousness response to this is to get angry, get revenge, or cultivate some form of hatred toward the agent of your adversity. But this response just amplifies your suffering. Responding to hatred with hatred perpetuates the hatred. Even externally, this will bring more adversity to your life in the form of negative consequences of your hatred. For example, if your neighbor dumps trash on your yard and then you dump trash on his yard, he will get angry and come up with another way to annoy you. Then you will get angry for that and come up with another way to get him back, and it will never end. We see this going on in the Middle East: violence being met with violence, which then causes more violence – a cycle of increasing violence. The result is hell on earth with no end in sight. Gang warfare follows the same twisted pattern. Everyone loses.

On one level we need justice and to preserve our well-being. If someone commits a crime or hurts you, steps should be taken. If it's serious, civil authorities might get involved. And you should try to take practical steps to prevent the incident from recurring. On the surface, you should do what has to be done to keep yourself and others out of harm's way.

But inside, you have to adopt a different attitude. Whatever happened was meant to happen. It's your new challenge. You should not waste time with lamentation or anger, much less feeling like a victim. You should simply accept the event, be grateful for the challenge, trust that it's for your growth and ultimate benefit, and deal with it in high consciousness, acting in karma-yoga. You should choose not to suffer, but instead to seek enlightenment.

If you get stuck with the first part, of not wasting time with lamentation or anger, then you need to use forgiveness. Forgiveness is in your toolbox to loosen up the lingering attachment to suffering and the latent desire to cultivate hatred or seek revenge. It is your last line of defense, cutting your ties to both the miserable event in question and the agent of that misery. If you don't do this, you'll remain attached to the misery and the agent and will continue to suffer.

Forgiveness doesn't mean you agree with what's been done or are saying it's okay, that it's no problem. Forgiveness means giving up the suffering by understanding that it was somebody else's action, not yours, and that you don't want to remain connected to it. It's you saying, "You did it; deal with the consequences. I'm not responsible for reminding you of your ill deeds."

Forgiveness is not for the benefit of the person who committed the mistake or crime; it's for your own sake. You're not being nice to please God or anyone else. You're forgiving because it's the only way you can become happy and free of negativity.

Actually, you shouldn't even need to forgive. Other people's actions based on negativity, lack of care, or outright aggression should not surprise you. It's just the way life is; the material world is like that. You want pure love and perfection? Then go back home, back to God, and join Him in eternal loving play in His abode with other perfected souls. Here in the material world, it's not going to happen. You've probably done your share of causing hurt, and whatever hurt you're feeling now is an echo of these actions in your past – the law of karma in action, helping you to become a better person. So waste no time lamenting or feeling angry. Take the necessary practical steps, as these are your dharma, but internally reject negativity. Don't fall into the trap of creating more suffering and negativity in reply to the suffering and negativity you've just received. You'll only perpetuate the cycle of suffering by doing this.

As a final meditation to help you cultivate the right mood in dealing with negativity from other people, I leave you with these wise words: "Every action you witness is either an expression of love or a cry for love." Responding to adversities caused by others with forgiveness and acting with love are the only ways to achieve a joyous and free state of mind.

Equanimity

The foremost quality of a yogi emphasized in the *Bhagavad-gita* is equanimity – to be equal, remaining the same, no matter what life throws at you. And since the *Bhagavad-gita* also tells us that the yogi has joyous and unlimited happiness, practicing equanimity means experiencing bliss, no matter the challenge.

Every situation is your opportunity to connect with God, in harmony with reality. Surface variations, variations of external material reality, are ultimately inconsequential for the transcendental soul. The soul, the real you, is operating at another frequency. The more you advance, the more you'll experience this. What the soul needs to be joyous has no connection with matter.

The most important way to gauge your spiritual advancement is to observe your level of equanimity. How stable is your well-being? How long does it take you to regain your harmony and inner peace when you're confronted with some type of adversity? Are you like a little row boat, thrown every which way by the stormy seas, or like a submarine, indifferent to storms on the surface?

Embrace the challenges life sends you as golden opportunities to practice equanimity and become stronger and more joyous.

CONCLUSION

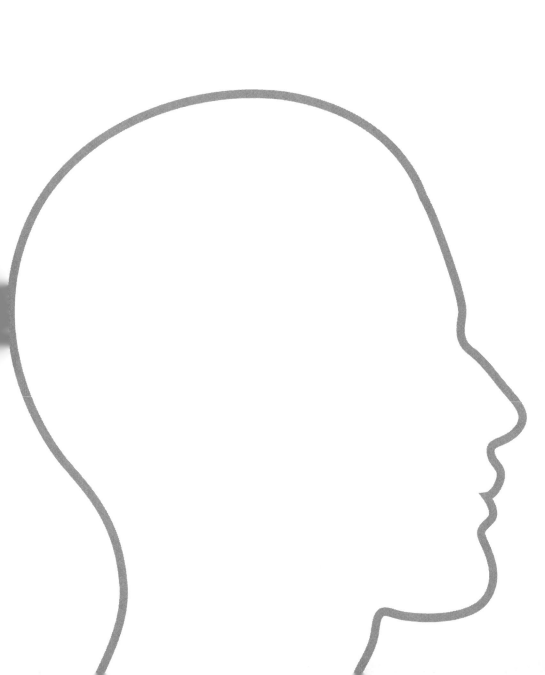

CONCLUSION

In its most profound sense, yoga is a path of self-improvement and self-realization. This path has traditionally focused on three areas: behavior, knowledge, and devotion.

The path of self-improvement is the same as that of self-realization. Self-realization is the final and natural aspect of dedicating yourself to making your life better. You need not commit to the spiritual and devotional practices, the final and most elevated aspects of the 3T Path, to start improving your life with the many other recommendations presented in this book. As you advance in each practice and process each new fact, your views on life are reshaped and your attractions shift. As you progress, your consciousness changes, just as it changed as you grew from a child to an adult. You should never underestimate the power of your transformation. If you follow this path of self-improvement, your state of mind down the road will be transformed in ways that might now seem inconceivable. Your brain will literally reshape itself, and the very notion of who you are, where you are, and what is in your best interest will be altered.

The 3T Path has five avenues of perfection: 1) mindfulness, 2) dharma, 3) inner peace, 4) jnana (knowledge), and 5) bhakti (devotion). Each of these is powerful in and of itself. Each has been put forward individually by different teachers and traditions, because each one is so effective. But you should not sell yourself short; you can and should make use of all of them at the same time. They complement each other; each makes the others easier to practice and makes your transformation faster and more effective. This is why the 3T Path is so powerful.

To further maximize your potential for transformation and to increase your general well-being, you can adjust various aspects of your lifestyle. These lifestyle adjustments help expand your consciousness, pacify your mind, and increase your physical well-being. They bring benefits to your mind, body, and spirit, and in some cases all of society and even our planet.

The power of the five avenues of perfection and the lifestyle suggestions laid out in the 3T Path are supported by an increasing body of scientific literature. Thousands of years of tradition and confirmation by modern science should serve as a powerful stimulus to increase your enthusiasm and determination to follow the 3T Path.

No advice or technique, no matter how good, will be of use if you don't put it into practice. Hundreds of facts and dozens of practices are presented throughout this book. To maximize your success and well-being, you should constantly, at every moment, be working on the five avenues of perfection of the 3T Path. The Key Concepts will lay down the foundation for your transformation and success.

The first Key Concept is "It's all about the mind." This is the basis of the whole path. You cannot be happy until you take control of your life experience from the inside out. You have unbelievable power to process reality in such a way as to be unlimitedly happy, joyful, serene, and loving. You're not a helpless passenger on a roller coaster ride, being forced to experience suffering, despair, and hopelessness. You can and should become the master of your life experience, and this book gives you all the knowledge and tools you need to make this start happening.

The second Key Concept is "The change of paradigm: life vs. fantasy." The key to achieving well-being and self-realization is to end the problematic and painful habit of living in the future. This is the source of your misery: your mind out of control, constantly fantasizing about what you need to be happy in the future and focused on the results of your activities. As you assume control of your mind, maintain your focus on the here and now. Align your mind with reality as it's happening at every moment, on what's the best thing you can do, and on doing that as well as you can. Feelings of unhappiness, anxiety, and incompleteness aren't satisfied by buying something, moving somewhere, or being with other people. The answer to all these painful negative states of mind lies in knowing how to live here and now, no matter what is going on in your life. Everything you need for an amazing life is inside you, within your grasp, right now.

The third Key Concept is "Beyond Victimhood; Taking Control." In order to assume command, you must assume full responsibility for the events in your life. You can't give others the power to make you happy or sad or demand that others fulfill your needs for attention and affection. Lamenting and blaming others for your poor life experience disempowers you and renders you incapable of achieving well-being. In the "Dealing with Life's Problems" section I explain in greater detail the means to deal with whatever life throws at you, and this Key Concept is the first step. Your focus should be exclusively on your actions and your state of mind. You must embrace the fact that the quality of your life depends exclusively on you.

The last Key Concept, "Karma-yoga," is the ancient yoga formula for how to live well and, more importantly, how to live spiritually. It's the technique for truly becoming a yogi, a living transcendentalist. In karma-yoga you rely on all five of the avenues of perfection of the 3T Path and apply them to every action you perform. Karma-yoga means to be in mindfulness, following your dharma, rejecting the fantasy paradigm, in inner peace, acting with wisdom and, most importantly, making your actions a loving offering to God.

All of this takes time, effort, and practice. It always comes back to how much you practice, how seriously you apply this to your life. No matter how wonderful or blissful a path or its goal may be, if you don't take to it seriously, it does you no good. A great and beautiful life in self-improvement and self-realization deserves your full commitment.

In order to make progress, it's essential to practice the 3T Method diligently. This will keep the flame alive and your consciousness transforming upward. The 3T Method is your daily dose of transcendence to keep you spiritually fit – the catalyst for your growth. Since time immemorial, all dedicated yogis have followed a daily practice (sadhana) to fuel their growth and transformation. The 3T Method is what drives your transformation on the 3T Path.

The world desperately needs change. The human race is destroying itself, the planet, and a multitude of other species. No combination of external changes will suffice. The world needs a spiritual awakening. It's already happening, though, and you can be a part of this positive change. A universal, non-sectarian, spiritual awakening is the only thing that can save us from a decline into further misery; it's our only hope for peace. You can be part of that change. Be the person you want others to be. Live the life you believe others should live for the benefit of all. Be an agent of harmony and light.

If the 3T Path is working for you, if you see value in it, or if it's helped you in any way, share it. Sharing is an act of love. It will benefit both you and those with whom you share it with. And the more you share this path, the more it becomes part of who you are and the deeper your realizations will be.

I can't describe how much bliss I've experienced in sharing this path for the past twenty-five years. God willing, I'll keep doing it until my last breath. I hope you have experienced as much joy in reading or hearing this book, as I've had in writing it. I pray that the 3T Path be of enormous benefit to you and that Krishna bless you with all the realizations He has given me – and much more.

THE 3T METHOD

For transformation to take place, there must be steady endeavor. In the yoga tradition there is the concept of sadhana: a daily practice for spiritual uplift-ment. Good intentions are not enough; there must be effort. And behind a general effort to advance and better yourself on many fronts, there must be a specific daily discipline driving your transformation onwards, day after day. The 3T Method is just that – a daily regime of transcendence and streng-thening of your mind and intelligence to help you take on the challenge of advancing in the five avenues of perfection on the 3T Path. I cannot empha-size enough the importance of this daily practice if you hope to fuel your transformation.

The 3Ts

The three *daily* transcendental practices are:

1. A minimum of twenty minutes of meditation, using the traditional mantra-meditation technique, called japa, with the maha-mantra,

2. Eating prasada, sacred karma-free food, and

3. A minimum of ten minutes cultivating transcendental knowledge by reading books from the suggested list.

Mantra Meditation – Japa

Meditation is the central practice of the yoga tradition. The whole process of self-improvement and self-realization is based on your ability to pacify and direct your mind. Your control and awareness of your mind is the key to your success in any spiritual path. And meditation is the supreme technique for achieving that control and awareness.

Meditation has been shown to literally alter the shape of your brain and bring about a wide range of physical and mental-health benefits. It goes beyond any personal beliefs. It's an amazing tool that no one should go without.

Meditation means to focus your mind on a single point. Different techniques focus on different points. In the Zen tradition it's literally a point (dot) in the wall in front of the meditator; in commercial yoga classes the point of focus is usually your breathing. But the most traditional form of meditation, recommended in the *Bhagavad-gita* and the *Yoga Sutras*, is mantra meditation, *japa* in Sanskrit. This is the technique I use and teach. I find it to be the most complete and beneficial form of meditation. Because the mantra contains God's names, japa brings all the benefits of other forms of meditation but with the advantages of helping you advance on the bhakti avenue of perfection and causing many subtle but powerful effects due to its transcendental sound vibration.

The mantra to be used is the Hare Krishna mantra:

Hare Krishna, Hare Krishna
Krishna Krishna, Hare Hare
Hare Rama, Hare Rama
Rama Rama, Hare Hare

This is also known as the *maha*-mantra, which means the "great" mantra, and it's widely recognized as the most powerful of all mantras in the yoga tradition.

The first word, *Hare*, is an invocation to Radha, the feminine aspect of God. *Krishna* is the name of God meaning "the all-attractive." And *Rama*, another holy name, means "the source of bliss." These are the three sacred sounds of the maha-mantra. Bhakti-yoga masters explain that the maha-mantra is a powerful means to establish connection with God in the mood of attaining loving service and divine protection.

For mantra meditation you should use meditation beads, japa-mala. If you don't yet have a mala, you can still get started by simply reciting the mantra. You can make a mala from a string, tying 27 or 54 knots. When you get a mala, you can just add it to your practice. Traditionally, these malas have 108 beads, but the number of beads makes no difference, and having a mala with 54 or even 27 beads can be more practical, especially for chanting on planes, trains, and in other public spaces.

Basic instructions on how to use your japa-mala:

1. Start with the first bead, at one end of the mala, holding it between your thumb and middle finger.
2. For each bead, softly chant the entire mantra: Hare Krishna, Hare Krishna, Krishna Krishna, Hare Hare / Hare Rama, Hare Rama, Rama Rama, Hare Hare.
3. After chanting on the last bead, at the other end of the mala, turn the beads around and go back in the opposite direction, continuing to recite the mantra once for each bead, until your allotted time for meditation is complete.
4. Use your meditation time for focusing exclusively on your spiritual dharma. Give yourself a break from all other dharmas. Forget for the moment that you're a mother, father, brother, employee, boss, or even an Earthling. Just focus on the sacred sound in complete mindfulness.

Traditionally, yogis chant a fixed number of mantras. When I was initiated, over 20 years ago, I vowed to chant the maha-mantra 1,728 times per day minimum, and I've kept that vow ever since, every single day. That's the equivalent of 16 times 108 beads. Each set of 108 beads is known as a round of japa. But I recommend that you first focus on a fixed amount of time, starting with a minimum of 20 minutes. If you advance enough to be doing more than an hour per day, then you can consider measuring it in rounds to chant these same 16 rounds a day minimum, as I do.

Additional tips for your mantra meditation:

1. Chant the mantra with attention being careful not to slur the words.

2. Chant without interruption. Create a flow of sacred sound.

3. Try to chant first thing in the morning, after waking and showering. It's especially effective before or around sunrise.

4. Fix your concentration on the sound of the mantra, not on the act of chanting it.

5. In the beginning it's common to chant very slowly, but you should speed up your chanting to enter more deeply into it. A rhythm of about 108 mantras in 5 minutes, without slurring the words, is a good goal.

6. Sit cross-legged with your back straight, shoulders relaxed, and buttocks raised off the ground on a cushion. If you can't sit cross-legged, sit on a chair with your feet placed firmly on the floor and your back straight, away from the back of the chair. Keep your eyes half-closed, resting your gaze about two meters in front of you. Breathe in through your nose and breathe out chanting. Your posture should be comfortable. The goal is to be relaxed but attentive.

7. Your mind will try to wander thinking about this and that. Try to ignore those thoughts and fix your mind on the mantra. This battle with your mind is the exercise of meditation. Don't get discouraged. As long as you're doing the exercise, you're benefitting. It's always working on some level, so never give up.

Eating Prasada

Prasada means "mercy." It's also the Sanskrit word used for sacred food. As the saying goes, "You are what you eat." In many ways, eating defines you. It certainly defines the shape of your body and your overall health. But it also defines your state of mind. Because eating is so fundamental, the yoga tradition gives it special attention.

As explained in the Karma-yoga Key Concept section of the 3T Path, every action should be carried out as an offering to God, as an act of love and recognition of the origin of everything. Food yoga, the practice of eating prasada, is the act of connecting your food to the divine, spiritualizing it. A yogi spiritualizes everything in his or her life, but a special conscious effort should be made to spiritualize your food, due to the importance of eating. The effort and practice of being aware – in the here and now, several times per day – of such a fundamental act as eating, and of making a spiritual connection in that act, helps keep your consciousness elevated throughout the day.

In karmic terms, not offering your food means that you take on the burden of the karma of your meal and the whole chain of production behind it. This is why there is a special note of caution by Krishna in the *Bhagavad-gita* on the importance of eating only prasada. Eating prasada brings you so much benefit; not eating prasada brings so many future troubles.

Only foods that will not negatively affect your consciousness can be offered. Foods that involve suffering, like meat or fish or eggs, or foods containing alcohol or other drugs, cannot be offered. If you're not yet in the standard of eating only such foods, you should still offer the part of your meal that is offerable.

Offering food is an act of your heart and your consciousness. It does not require external rituals or actions. It does not need more than a few seconds. If you can and want, however, you can ritualize it and spend more time in the act of offering, as a form of meditation in bhakti. You can chant the maha-mantra a few times softly or in thought. You can get to the point of having special plates used exclusively for offering food on a home altar. But what really counts is your love, your bhakti, in the act of offering the food to God (Krishna).

Basic guidelines regarding prasada:

1. Don't taste the food before offering it.

2. If you're eating at a restaurant, offer the food on your plate before eating.

3. Offer food only once. If you buy a loaf of bread, for instance, offer it all and then it's prasada. There's no need to offer it again every time you take a slice.

4. If you forget to offer your food, don't give up. Just try to remember at your next meal. In time, it will become second nature.

If you feel up to it, there is an additional practice known as the ekadasi vrata, or just ekadasi. *Ekadasi* means "the eleventh." It refers to the eleventh day of the moon cycle. As you may know, the moon waxes for approximately fourteen days and wanes for another fourteen in its cycle from full moon to new moon. The eleventh day of each cycle is known as ekadasi. Those who practice ekadasi don't eat any kind of grain or legume, such as beans, wheat, chickpea, peas, corn, soy, and rice. Everything else can be eaten normally. This requires extra mindfulness throughout the day in regard to the act of eating, which in itself is a great practice. Some people do full fasts on ekadasi. Traditionally, ekadasis are days to try to increase your spiritual focus and activity.

The perfection of prasada is to cook and offer pure healthy vegetarian foods with love, and then to eat while maintaining that loving connection. That's food yoga to its highest extent. For more on food yoga, I recommend Paul Rodney Turner's book *Food Yoga*.

Cultivating Transcendental Knowledge

Information leads to transformation. Our most dangerous enemy is ignorance, because lack of knowledge leads to confusion and foolish, useless, painful activities. To become enlightened, you need the light of knowledge to dispel the darkness of ignorance. If I had to pick one of these three daily practices as the most important for beginners, I would choose this one, because if you pursue it properly, in due time you'll adopt the other two daily practices and adjust all your habits and mental processes for the better. This is the one practice that I've seen give the highest probability of success and stamina on this path. Those who cultivate transcendental knowledge are sure to achieve high levels of transformation.

The practice is very simple. Just dedicate at least ten minutes every day to reading or hearing the books listed below, going through them in the order listed. This is therapy – bibliotherapy. The knowledge will transform you as it opens new horizons, removes your doubts, brings you clarity, and bestows on you increasing wisdom. This practice will help you advance in the fourth avenue of perfection of the 3T Path: jnana, as well as the fifth, bhakti.

Books (in reading [or hearing] order):

1. *The 3T Path*, Giridhari Das

2. *A Comprehensive Guide to Bhagavad-Gita: With Literal Translation*, H.D. Goswami

3. *Patanjali's Yoga Sutras: Revolution*, Giridhari Das

4. *Krishna: The Beautiful Legend of God: Srimad Bhagavata Purana*, Edwin F. Bryant

5. *Swami in a Strange Land: How Krishna Came to the West: The Life of A.C. Bhaktivedanta Swami Prabhupada*, Joshua M. Greene

6. *Sri Isopanishad,* A.C. Bhaktivedanta Swami Prabhupada

7. *Bhagavad-gita As It Is,* A.C. Bhaktivedanta Swami Prabhupada

8. *Teachings of Lord Caitanya,* A.C. Bhaktivedanta Swami Prabhupada

9. *The Nectar of Devotion,* A.C. Bhaktivedanta Swami Prabhupada

10. *Krsna, The Supreme Personality of Godhead,* A.C. Bhaktivedanta Swami Prabhupada

11. *The Nectar of Instruction,* A.C. Bhaktivedanta Swami Prabhupada

12. *Srila Prabhupada Lilamrta,* Satsvarupa Dasa Goswami

13. *Srimad-Bhagavatam,* A.C. Bhaktivedanta Swami Prabhupada

14. *Caitanya Caritamrta,* A.C. Bhaktivedanta Swami Prabhupada

Tips for making the most of this practice:

1. Set a fixed time of your day for this practice. Make it a special sacred moment of at least ten minutes when you can concentrate on just this task.

2. Don't worry about understanding everything. Don't get hung up on one fact or explanation. Keep reading. You'll see that everything is internally coherent and you'll be able to make sense of it all once you have absorbed enough information.

3. Don't think you have to practice everything you read. There will be a lot of information and a lot of examples of great yogis dating back through thousands of years. Many different practices and recommendations will be mentioned. Stay focused on the recommendations and practices of the 3T Path.

4. These books, especially the great classics by A.C. Bhaktivedanta Swami Prabhupada, get better and easier to understand when you read them a second or third time. They are very deep, and as you advance and gain deeper levels of consciousness, you'll be able to absorb deeper meanings and realizations.

APPENDIX

How to Introduce Changes in Your Life

There are many techniques for introducing new habits and changes to your life, and each can be powerful, but there are three that, when combined, are unbeatable: the Baby Start, Zorro Circles, and the Kaizen Principle.

Baby Start

The hardest part of starting something new is just starting it! We are trying to introduce something that's not already part of our lives. Neuroscience explains that new things activate our apprehension and resistance. We naturally want to keep things as they are, on automatic. It's easier on our brains and requires less effort. Doing something we've never done before requires the use of different parts of our brain, which demands more energy and increases our heartrate, our blood pressure, and the size of our irises, along with other physiological effects. We're not conscious of them, but the result is simple: we don't like to engage in such mental effort. So doing something new and creating a new habit is a really big deal.

To overcome this resistance to the new, dial down your effort to a minimum with a "Baby Start." Any start is a big step; so make the start so small that you can't possibly rebel against it, even unconsciously. Make it laughably small—as small as you can imagine it. The more resistance you've felt regarding a new habit, the more you're procrastinating to avoid it, the smaller you have to make the starting point. The concept is simple: diminish the obstacle to the point it's no longer an obstacle.

For example, if you want to become vegetarian but don't know where to start, you can determine something like this: "Tomorrow, I'll just leave the last morsel of meat on my plate." There! Easy, right? Just one morsel less tomorrow. You have now officially started on your path to a meat-free diet!

Are you trying to get your house organized but can't? Choose something tiny. Organize (and keep organized) just one square meter of the house, or half a shelf. Want to start exercising again? Start with a proposal that the next day you'll do one single squat. That's it!

For bigger or more complex projects, like writing a book or getting a new career, divide the task into a sequence of small steps. For example: "Tomorrow I'll dedicate five minutes of my day to search for different suggestions on how to write a book." Or write down five things you'd like to include in the book. And then continue like that, creating easily achievable goals to keep your work progressing. Whenever you feel that you've stalled, break it down further, make it even easier.

This will make it so easy to start that you just can't refuse. And mentally, it's a huge gain: "I've begun—I'm on my way!"

Zorro Circles

It's a basic human need to feel that you have some control over your life and environment. Whatever the field of endeavor, we need to feel that our actions cause a reaction. When we lose this connection, we lose motivation.

We can become overwhelmed in any area of our life. The loss of control can become so great that we may feel that everything is in chaos. At this point, we just give up. This dynamic can certainly affect one's quest for self-improvement and self-realization.

With Zorro Circles we address this issue by finding an area where we can again assume full control, to regain our confidence and motivation.

The secret is to narrow your focus down to something you can control, a small part of a greater objective. Once you experience control over that small part, you can expand the circle to encompass a little more. This will keep you motivated and strong, directly experiencing that your actions are causing the right reactions.

At this point, you are solidly motivated and in full control of your Zorro Circle.

If you slip, you reduce the circle again and gradually regain your footing. The aim is to preserve a sense of control. How large or small a part of the objective makes you preserve this feeling of control is there for you to adjust.

In time, you will be able to expand the circle to cover the whole objective in question.

The Kaizen Principle

Kaizen is a principle developed in Japanese industry after World War II. It's brilliant in its simplicity: Try do things just a little better. That's it. Just the tiniest bit better than before.

Whatever was being done, the Japanese industrialists would ask, "Can this be done just a little better?" And by doing this, they perfected production lines, factories, products, and customer service, and in just a few decades rebuilt their country from ruins to a powerful modern nation.

In neurological terms, the concept is similar to the Baby Start. By advancing ever so slightly, you don't trigger discomfort or insecurity; you disarm any conscious or unconscious resistance.

You build up your new habit on a secure basis.

Putting the Three Together

Now let's put the three together. First think of the easiest possible beginning to your new habit—a Baby Start. Remember, it has to be so easy and simple that you can't say no to it. This is your first Zorro Circle, where you'll feel in full control.

Next, applying the Kaizen Principle, pick just the tiniest increment of what you're doing and try to improve or extend it by just the smallest amount.

For example, in the case of becoming vegetarian, you can reduce your meat consumption by just one more morsel each day, or even each week. If it's about keeping your house tidy, try to keep two square meters tidy, or the whole shelf instead of just half the shelf. If it's about beginning an exercise regimen, the next day go from doing a single squat to two.

Keep everything really smooth and easy. No stress. Just one tiny increment at a time. Your Zorro Circle will expand, and you'll feel secure and in control of the experience. This is your guiding principle: security and control. It determines your commitment to change.

Hit a snag? New habit interrupted? Start again, retracing the practice to a level of commitment you're comfortable with, as tiny as you like. Find that sweet spot of security and control and start growing again from there.

Your practice will soon become habit, and before you know it you'll have conquered your resistance and achieved your desired change. Once it's a habit, you're home free. It becomes automatic, using a different part of your brain, thus requiring less energy. It's just you doing your thing.

Then you're ready to acquire a new habit, small step by small step perfecting and bettering yourself. And this will increase your growth and sense of well-being, with the satisfaction of improving your life day after day.

Transform with Kindness and Forgiveness

If we're too hard on ourselves when learning new habits or trying to become a better person, we decrease our chances of success. This has to do with a curious fact about the workings of our brains.

When we feel threatened, we naturally seek shelter. Our brain, however, cannot distinguish reality from thoughts. An external threat or harsh criticism registers the same as one that exists only in our head, internally.

This means that you can hurt yourself with your thoughts, without your conscious knowledge reacting physiologically and neurologically to perceived threats. One reaction is to retreat to our zone of comfort, our mental space of security and familiarity. The zone of comfort includes who you are now and what you do. It's not the new-and-improved version of yourself you're trying to build, and by going there, you reduce your chances for change and growth.

Researcher Kelly McGonigal describes a study that confirms this reaction is self-criticism and -incrimination. Women trying to lose weight who received messages of self-forgiveness ate half as many sweets as women who did not get such messages. The same with studies of people trying to stop smoking or gambling, as well as those with serious problems of procrastination. Dr. McGonigal concluded that guilt and stress are enemies of self-control and thus counter-productive factors in the process of transformation.

What is a message of self-forgiveness? Instead of being hard on yourself, try being gentle. The best and simplest way of doing this is to pretend you're talking to your best friend after he or she tells you about a failure to stick to his or her goals. If your friend told you, for instance, that he or she cannot meditate every day, how would you react? With harsh criticism, arousing sentiments of shame and guilt? I hope not! Most likely you'd respond with something like, "Oh, no problem. What's important is that you're trying every day. We have good and bad days. Try again tomorrow!"

Well, you should treat yourself this way, too—with self-forgiveness. By being kind and gentle with yourself, you will expand your comfort zone and feel secure and encouraged to grow and transform. You'll feel better and be able to attain your goals more efficiently.

Graphic Visualization of the 3T Path

With the help of my friend and student, Bruna Bindu Lima, I designed a graphic representation of the 3T Path to show how the different elements fit together. Here it is:

The process starts with the transmission of knowledge or wisdom—jnana. Knowledge can change your life. The basic principle is that if we're making mistakes in life, it's because we lack the knowledge. If we suffer, it's because we're doing it wrong, and we're doing it wrong because we don't know how to do it right. Thus, if we are empowered with knowledge and wisdom, we'll do it right, and as a result, we'll be happy. Specifically, yoga aims to provide us with deep knowledge about the nature of the soul, God, and the hidden truths of nature, such as the Law of Karma and the existence of the modes of material nature. This allows us to access the spiritual dimension of our mental map and opens our eyes to the divine nature of reality.

When we properly understand jnana, we naturally develop bhakti—loving devotion to God. If we pursue our study of God seriously, we'll focus our attention on Krishna, the sweetest and most intimate personal expression of the Lord.

Jnana and bhakti form the self-realization part of the path and are the two most advanced aspects of yoga. Because of that, they are the two that most deeply affect our lives, but they are also the most difficult to access. In fact, it's hard even for people to become interested in them. In order to advance in jnana and bhakti, you need a systematic effort. That's why I present the 3T Method, a daily practice—sadhana—to grant access to these higher levels of the 3T Path. Without a daily sustained effort, it's simply not possible to advance along these avenues of perfection.

Surrounding the spiritual part of the path—jnana and bhakti—we find the other three avenues of perfection, the self-improvement elements of our practice: mindfulness, dharma, and inner peace. They don't require belief or spiritual vision. They don't even require much deep thought. They provide practical advice with immediate and undeniable impact. It's enough to hear them explained for any person to recognize their validity and the need to put them into practice. These three avenues of self-improvement contain techniques and knowledge that quickly bring us relief, solving life's common day-to-day problems. It's the stuff we're all looking for, no matter our age, race, sex, nationality, or religion.

The key change is bringing our mind to the here and now, living the paradigm of reality. This is the portal to all higher states of consciousness. And more specifically, it's about your mind staying focused on your dharma, on the best you have to offer at any given moment. This determines your happiness. There is no getting around this. Without living in the here and now, focused on your dharma, life becomes the mess you know all too well: an almost constant state of anxiety, frustration, and confusion, interspersed with the illusory happiness of dreaming of a better life and the brief respite offered by entertainment or, worse, drugs. But if you put all the elements of the 3T Path into practice and live the reality paradigm, with your mind in the here and now, you will experience ever-deeper feelings of wellbeing, joy, peace, harmony, and love.

Even for those focused on practicing self-realization, it's still necessary to practice the three avenues of self-improvement. For example, you can't have a true spiritual experience of communion with God if your mind is still in the fantasy paradigm and far from the here and now. Not only is your common mundane reality happening in this very moment, but so too is divine reality. Similarly, you can't follow the spiritual path without living your dharma. Dharma is the bridge between matter and spirit. Living your dharma is living your purpose here on earth, at each moment. First we need to be connected with our practical essence—our physical, emotional, and social reality—to guarantee a firm connection to our transcendental nature.

Thus, we must practice the complete path. This is one of my core messages. If you're a spiritualist, don't ignore the need to practice mindfulness, to live your dharma, and to take care of your emotions. If you're already practicing self-improvement, trying to live a better life, don't ignore the need for self-realization, for practicing a daily set of spiritual practices, such as the 3T Method.

Our lifestyle choices are placed around the five avenues of perfection in this graphic representation. They determine our ability to even become interested in self-improvement and self-realization. And once you are interested, these choices determine your potential for putting in practice and absorbing the knowledge to progress in these five avenues of perfection. As such, they are the backdrop for your life experience.

One interesting detail revealed by this graphic presentation of the 3T Path is that all of the external aspects represented by everything outside of the circles jnana and bhakti, is totally confirmed by modern science. Mindfulness has been validated by over ten thousand scientific studies. The practices and knowledge contained in the section of inner peace are all confirmed by psychology and neuroscience. And the avenue of perfection of dharma—the importance of living your values, searching for meaning, seeking intrinsic objectives, and living your nature—is being studied by science and becoming increasingly valued in the corporate world.

Jnana can be proved by reason. By applying your reason and engaging in critical thinking, you can confirm how this transcendental knowledge makes your life easier to understand and thus easier to live. It gives you the ability to understand all of life's experiences in a rational manner. In short, advancement along the avenue of perfection of jnana provides you with answers to those questions modern science cannot tackle.

Bhakti, the highest aspect of yoga, can be confirmed only by direct perception. The process takes you to the point of having the experience of direct communion with God. You can't prove it to someone else, only offer testimony to it. And there is no scarcity of testimonies. Billions of people, throughout history and in every corner of the world, have testified to their contact with divine reality. Scientific studies have proven the benefits of religion, and there are logical and philosophical arguments supporting the existence of God. But none of this proves the reality of bhakti to someone who hasn't yet activated his or her own devotional spirituality. The experience of loving devotion to God—bhakti—must be personally and directly experienced.

Everything contained in the 3T Path is real and effective. You can verify it yourself—by reason or, better yet, through practice. The process is complete and contains many parts, each of which will bring you benefits and help you practice the others. This graphic visualization of the process as a whole can help you see how it all fits together and inspire you to put it all in practice, step by step, as described in this book.

Conclusion

Nothing of value in life can be accomplished without dedication and persistence, and this is most certainly true when it comes to self-improvement and self-realization. The 3T Method works. Try it and you'll see. But you have to practice every day. If you fail one day, it becomes more likely that you'll fail the next. If you fail two days in a row, it becomes somewhat unlikely that you'll even try again. The first twenty-one days are the toughest. That's the average time it takes for something to become a habit, which the 3T Method should become. After twenty-one days, you'll feel the positive effects of the daily practices making it easier to keep doing it. Just like a plane or rocket requires more fuel to take off than to cruise, you will need extra effort and determination to get going on your path of transformation. So use everything you can to gain traction on this path.

You have the tools and you have the knowledge. Now it's up to you to put them to use. The power is in your hands.

ABOUT THE AUTHOR

Giridhari Das, or Giri for short is a self-help and spiritual teacher, author, and speaker. He has been practicing bhakti-yoga, the yoga of devotion, and working with self-development for over 20 years. His mission is to present the 3T Path, a transformative process to meet and transcend the challenges of life in the 21st Century, based on the knowledge of yoga found in both ancient Sanskrit texts and the latest research in the fields of positive psychology and neuroscience. The 3T Path can be easily understood and applied as a means of self-improvement and self-realization in the world today.

Giri was born in Prague in 1969 as Gustavo Dauster, the son of a Brazilian diplomat. A few years later he and his family returned to Brazil, where he stayed until he was 9 years old. Then he moved to London where he lived for the next 8 years and studied at the American High School. Later he spent a year in the USA at Brown University and, after permanently moving back to Brazil, completed his degree in economics.

His career was just beginning when he was introduced to the bhakti path through a business contact. He spoke to him about Krishna consciousness, and his wife gave him a copy of the Bhagavad-gita As It Is. He was impressed with the knowledge found there and soon become seriously committed to the path, the daily practices and the studies.

In 1993, he met his spiritual master, Hridayananda Das Goswami Acharyadeva, and after developing a close relationship with him as his disciple, he took formal initiation in 1998, receiving from him the spiritual name, Giridhari Das.

For many years, he participated actively in ISKCON in various positions of administration and leadership in Brazil. For 10 years he was in charge of the Brazilian branch of the BBT, the publishing house of the Hare Krishna movement, and after that he served for several years as president of the governing body of ISKCON Brazil.

Today he owns and runs a Yoga Resort called Pandavas Paradise in Chapada dos Veadeiros in the highland plateaus of central Brazil. He lives there with his wife, Charana Renu Dasi (Rhiannon Dauster), and his two young sons, Bryn Govardhana and Macsen Krishna. He met Charana in Wales in 2007 while touring with his spiritual master. She has also been practicing and teaching bhakti--yoga since 1999.

He enjoys teaching students and guests at their yoga resort and at other spiritual centers in Brazil and around the world, and for many years he has been teaching and guiding people through email, but more recently he began to feel the need to reach out to a larger audience and in 2014 started a YouTube channel for that purpose. He currently records videos for two YouTube channels in Portuguese and one in English. He has also published four books on yoga and self-realization in Portuguese and The 3T Path in English.

The focus of his teaching is the 3T Path, a systematic, modern presentation of the ancient path of self-improvement and self-realization in yoga and Krishna consciousness. He developed the 3T Path after many years of dedicated study and practice, to share his experience and realizations in bhakti, and to address the needs and challenges of people today.

THE 3T PATH REVIEWS

"This impressive book from Giridhari Das makes it clear why he is a spiritual internet star. This systematic, eloquent book provides valuable guidance for those seeking serious spiritual progress."
– *Hridayananda Das Goswami* –

"You wrote a book which offers valuable information, interesting anecdotes and historical data, and ends with a surprisingly complete description of Krishna and devotional service. Quite an achievement."
– *Joshua M. Greene (Yogesvara Das)* –

"If you are seeking an insightful and meaningful spiritual experience, in a language you can understand, The 3T Path is a must read! Giridhari Das has taken what is an exhaustive and expansive body of spiritual and commonly misunderstood knowledge, and laid it all out in a simple, practical and easy to understand way. Just by reading it, your life will become better and happier!"
– *Mahavira Das* –

"Giridhari Das' The 3T Path expertly bridges ancient yoga traditions and contemporary Western society. Giridhari makes philosophical ideas accessible to both curious beginners and experienced practitioners and gives us clear, practical directions on how we can apply yoga practices and principles to our everyday lives."
– *Dr. Carl Herzig, Professor of English, St. Ambrose University* –

"I can say that I enjoyed every word and instruction in this magnificent work. It impels us to think upon life's purpose in an objective and thankful way."
– *Enéas Guerriero (Iswara dasa), author, speaker, life and spirit coach* –

"In this book, Giridhari Das offers an invaluable present to humanity. Works such as this are true treasures – manifestations of divine compassion in the service of dharma, the higher purpose. I would also say that The 3T Path is a practical survival guide in difficult times."
– *Sri Prem Baba* –

"a well thought and important book"
– *Ithamar Theodor (Isvara Krsna Das)* –

"[an] amazing and very enlightening book."
– *Pedro Rodrigues* –

"More than a reading, it is a life changing experience."
– *Grady Harp* –

"I'm loving the easy and straight foward language."
– *Gisele Rodrigues* –

"An important and well thought book."
– *Ithamar Theodor (Isvara Krsna Das)* –

"You can't stop reading it. The 3T Path is a book that connects Yoga wisdom to your day-to-day life, with tools and practical examples that show how to keep your mind healthy, focused on the here and now."
– *Taila Roncon* –

"Cure and nourishment for your mind, soul, and body... an inspiring book."
– *Meg* –

"It is a book to have in your bedside, meaning, to be constantly read."
— *Sergio Mendonça* —

"The reading is resonating greatly in my life. I strongly recommend!!!"
— *Márcia Uehara* —

"An enlightening book!"
— *Shani K.* —

"With an everyday speech, useful examples and deep understanding of yoga history, Giridhari Das offers an spiritual toolbox to be used anytime."
— *Dotrazn* —

"It is a wonderful book. A great introduction to mindfulness and meditation to newcomers."
— *Talia Wong* —

"A perfect foundation to every reader, independently of the currently level of knowledge regarding yoga."
— *Jill Baker* —

"It is impressive how The 3T Path shows us the power of transformation that bhakti-yoga has, using an everyday speech, straightforward language and that touches our mind and spirit, to be pratcticed wholly in our day-to-day life and that conects us to ourselves and God. Gratittude for the gift."
— *Roberto Moura* —

Amazon Reviews

"It is more than a book – it is a life-altering experience."
— *Grady Harp* —

"Healing and sustenance for your mind, soul and body... an inspiring book"
– *Meg* –

"This is very enlightening!"
– *Shani K.* –

"By applying clear language, helpful examples, and an thorough grasp of the history of yoga, Giridhari Das offers a spiritual toolkit that can be used at any time."
– *Dotrazn* –

"This is a wonderful book. Great intro for newcomers to mindfulness and meditation practices."
– *Talia Wong* –

"Perfect background for all readers regardless of current knowledge level of yoga."
– *Jill Baker* –

"A great read! I absolutely enjoyed this book by Giridhari Das."
– *Jengel* –

"Amazing book and life changing, full of good advice and philosophical timeless wisdom! I highly recommend it!"
– *Radha Krishna* –

"A life saver!"
– *Ivan Llobet* –

"Excellent roadmap for the Bhakti path. This book has a neat and clear step-by-step process for one to engage in authentic Bhakti Yoga. The practical, organized, and simplified format was a welcome contrast to some books which are too complex for beginners."
— Billy Kubina Jr. —

"This book is incredible! It really changed my life and will change yours too."
— Anonymous —